ZERO POINT

ZERO POINT

Moments Beyond Conscious Thought

Thomas Paul Emerson

INNERSIGHTS
DANA POINT, CALIFORNIA 92629

© 2000 Thomas Paul Emerson. Printed and bound in the United States of America. All rights reserved. No part of this book may be reproduced or transmitted in any form or by any means, electronic or mechanical, including photocopying, recording, or by an information storage and retrieval system—except by a reviewer who may quote brief passages in a review to be printed in a magazine or newspaper—without permission in writing from the publisher. For information, please contact us at 800-983-4445, or visit our Web site, www.new-age.org.

Although the author and publisher have made every effort to ensure the accuracy and completeness of information contained in this book, we assume no responsibility for errors, inaccuracies, omissions, or any inconsistency herein. Any slights of people, places, or organizations are unintentional.

First printing 2000

ISBN 0-9674671-9-5

LCCN 99-97118

ATTENTION CORPORATIONS, UNIVERSITIES, COLLEGES, AND PROFESSIONAL ORGANIZATIONS: Quantity discounts are available on bulk purchases of this book for educational purposes. Special books or book excerpts can also be created to fit specific needs.

CONTENTS

Section One: INTRODUCTION

Chapter 1 ● *Life in a New Age* 9

Chapter 2 ● *Opening Doors of Perception* 25

Chapter 3 ● *The Art of Meditation* 33

Chapter 4 ● *Spiritualized Sex* 45

Chapter 5 ● *Life After Death* 57

Section Two: QUESTIONS

Chapter 6 ● *Do You Know Where Your Mind Is?* 69

Chapter 7 ● *Where Is God Today?* 75

Chapter 8 ● *Morality in the Twenty-First Century* 85

Chapter 9 ● *Love New Age Style* 93

Chapter 10 ● *Self-Growth* 99

Chapter 11 ● *Destiny and Freedom* 111

Chapter 12 ● *What About Science and Religion?* 119

Chapter 13 ● *UFOs, ESP, and Voodoo?* 125

● References 129

● Index 131

ZERO POINT

Introduction

*To Your
Silent Witness*

INTRODUCTION

It was 1968. The Beatles had just gone to see Maharishi Mahesh Yogi at his mountain retreat in Rishikesh, and the Western world was about to be introduced to one of its first New Age messiahs. While at Maharishi's, John Lennon and Paul McCartney worked on songs for their *White Album*,[1] the songs of which would soon rank among the most popular anthems for a new generation. The Woodstock festival and man's first walk on the moon were just one year away. This was an exciting time in American history—and perhaps one of the most poignant—in what was later to be coined a New Age.

I was a teenager then, and Eastern religion, hippies, and rock and roll were a sign of the times. I grew up in California where I found myself surrounded by a New Age generation. I went to conferences and expositions, became a vegetarian, studied astrology, went barefoot, and even had a pyramid over my bed for a while. A Christian since childhood, I found myself fascinated by Eastern religion. The messages of Krishnamurti, Yogananda, Muktananda, Ram Dass, and the like were by this time reaching millions. Christ, Ramakrishna, Krishna, Patanjali, and Shankara were among the great teachers who influenced me. I used to go to Ojai, California, to see Krishnamurti, whom I considered my guru.

By the early seventies, I began to study meditation and yoga. After twelve years of practice, I became initiated into a form of meditation called Kundalini Yoga, by a spiritual master from India. During this meditation I felt a sensation moving up my spine to a point between my eyebrows, which he called "the third eye." This energy is known as the Kundalini.

Pilgrimage

Meditation took me to a spot where I was momentarily beyond the concerns of my life, and all I knew was there was so much more to life than what I was aware of. During the mid-1970s and the 1980s, I went to many places trying to understand as much as I could about myself. I wanted to see through as many layers of myself as I could, but there always seemed to be another layer underneath. Mahatma Gandhi once wrote, "If you would swim on the bosom of the ocean of Truth you must reduce yourself to a zero."[2]

Traveling helped me to get out of my more routine way of thinking and to reduce myself toward zero. I traveled around the United States, Canada, Mexico, Central America, then Europe, India, and Nepal, on a sort of spiritual pilgrimage. I wanted to see through myself and see what others could see. I visited many people, places, and temples. I lived sometimes as a homeless person, roaming from place to place with a knapsack. I slept in the bushes beside the road, and I rummaged through trash bins behind supermarkets. For a couple of years, I hitchhiked through North America, talking to many people as I rode with them in their cars. Occasionally, I worked as a day laborer or at a temporary job to get enough money so I could continue traveling.

I stayed on a Indian reservation in Arizona with a spiritual teacher. She taught me many of the spiritual ways of her people. While in India I met a revered yogi, whose message was so simple and yet sublime. Most of all, I learned the significance of devotion, and how important it is to pray and to think of God. I also spoke to many Brahmins, sadhus, and teachers in various parts of India.

Introduction

When I returned to the United States, I felt like I didn't quite fit in. I quietly pursued Eastern religion and astrology, and before long I met others who were interested in these subjects. Eventually, I started a part-time business of astrology and hypnosis.

The Late 1980s

It seemed much of the hype of the counterculture was settling down, and some of the more commercial fads were quickly fading as the mainstream began to take a more serious look at this new fast-growing population. Even the larger bookstores were now dedicating whole sections to "New Age" books. After my pilgrimage I decided to explore a field more related to the investigation of consciousness. It would be several years, however, before I eventually was drawn to the study of hypnosis. What caught my attention at first was when I heard several therapists had reported their patient's had spoken of past lives while under hypnosis. One of my favorite books at the time was *Many Lives Many Masters*[3] by Brian L. Weiss, M.D.

As a boy I was hypnotized several times by my best friend's father, who was trying to help me increase my self-confidence. These early experiences showed me hypnosis and meditation are extremely similar, if not identical. I found that what is called a guided meditation is the same as what is called hypnosis. And self-hypnosis is the same as what people call meditation. When someone guides you into meditation, this is actually the same as someone hypnotizing you. Both result in a trance. The major difference is that usually in meditation you are not trying to specifically change anything. Most people meditate to enjoy inner peace, reflection, and silence, whereas in hypnosis the intention is usually to change a certain habit or belief.

Hypnotherapy

At the beginning of the 1990s, I became a certified hypnotherapist, and then eventually a neuro-linguistic practitioner. I opened an office and it wasn't long before I began to receive calls from people who wanted to use hypnosis to remember a previous lifetime. In the beginning, I had my doubts about whether I was actually going to be able to guide anyone into a past life. In the years that followed, however, I guided many people into what they believed were recollections of another lifetime. One thing became clear: These people believed there was a direct correlation between their spiritual circumstances in a previous life and their current life situation. They explained how their previous life had in some way "sowed the seeds" for their present experiences. They saw many of the same people with them in various lifetimes. I soon realized being born again was like waking up in the morning, after a night's rest, and just continuing your life.

This Book

Over the years, clients and students encouraged me to write about my experiences. This book is not about past life stories but about the journey I have experienced during my past twenty-five years.

In one of my favorite books, *The Prophet*, Kahlil Gibran writes:

> *Like the ocean is your God-self;*
> *It remains forever undefiled.*
> *And like the ether it lifts but the winged.*
> *Even like the sun is your god-self;*
> *It knows not the ways of the mole nor seeks it the*
> *   holes of the serpent.*
> *But your god-self dwells not alone in your being.*
> *Much in you is still man, and much in you is not*
> *   yet man,*

> *But a shapeless pigmy that walks asleep in the mist searching for its own awakening.*[4]

The message that underlies this book is that Gibran's "God-self" is the Spirit in each of us. The pigmy-self, or our ego, is an aging person who's born, grows old, and dies—but our Spirit lasts forever. The Spirit watches over our life, and provides us with an awareness of existence, and ourselves if we will just quietly listen. Furthermore, what we call "right" or "good" from a spiritual perspective is what we do out of love.

I want to share an awareness that promises a common ground between science and religion. My parents are kind, honest, and loving people, but very traditional. I remember one day I came home from elementary school and told my mother I had learned about the theory of evolution. She told me that science was definitely wrong about this theory, and that God had created man out of dust in just one day. I was confused and struggled to understand whether I should believe science or our church. I believe each of us knows deep inside, just as I did as a child, there is a degree to which they are both right. However, if either denies the other, then it will be partially wrong. Science, for example, can't prove that something like Spirit exists. A physical instrument can only measure something else that is physical—like a camera only takes a picture of something visible through its lens. Meanwhile, the church denies the evidence of science, because science explains things we didn't know about 2,000 years ago. This book shares a common ground between science and religion.

In the first five chapters we'll take a look at several of the most popular New Age subjects today, such as prophecies, Zen, yoga, meditation, Tantra, near death experiences (NDE), and past life regression (PLR). In the last eight chapters we'll look at some questions regarding these subjects.

It is my sincere wish that this book shed light on some of the spiritual issues today that can become clouded during these changing times.

People in India, after being introduced to another person, say, *Namaste,* which means "to that which is sacred in you, from that which is sacred in me." *"Namaste!"*

—Thomas Paul Emerson

Life in a New Age

As we enter the twenty-first century—and a new millennium—we see a mind-boggling acceleration in technology. The world is changing faster and faster every day! We seem to be entering a new age of belief and understanding. Globally, we're becoming a more interdependent world, and there is more a blending of cultures and traditions.

Nowhere has this cultural blending been more evident than in the United States. One such influx was that of Eastern religion in the 1970s. At the time many believed this new way of thinking was just a cult, but by the 1980s, mainstream America was incorporating many elements of this new philosophy into their daily lives. It soon became somewhat trendy, with lots of books on yoga and health management. It wasn't long before bookstores carried an amazing assortment of Eastern books, herbal remedies, incense, and music. Despite some of its more "far-out" or "way-out" proponents, this cultural phenomenon has united the Western emphasis on social responsibility with the Eastern science of self-realization. At the heart of this collaboration is a truly fascinating blend of lifestyle, philosophy, religion, and medicine.

As the world seems to grow smaller, and technology continues to boggle the imagination, we have also developed the means for mass destruction. As earth's population soars, there are more people for all of us to get along with. Researchers expect our world population to double between 1975 and the year 2017.[5] Our current population increases by 90 million people each year. By the year 2017 it is estimated we may be sharing the planet with as many as 8 billion people! We also now have the technology to solve some of our worst problems, like hunger, war, and pollution. So whether you think the "end of the world" is right around the corner, or a New Age with a more unified world—one thing is sure, we're all going to find out together! For peace to prevail, it is vital we develop a strong spirit of brotherly and sisterly love. Each of us can do our own part, by serving and developing a sincere acceptance of others, regardless of another's skin color, cultural differences, or religion. The change begins in our own minds, and in our homes, neighborhoods, and schools. We must be willing to pitch in to help others to help themselves.

The concern for world peace reached a new height in the 1940s with the advent of the nuclear bomb. In the aftermath of that deadly display, it was clear world peace was the key to our survival. Some say this was the beginning of the New Age generation. The first of several landmark books was published in 1946: Peace of Mind[6] by Rabbi Joshua Liebman was on the bestseller's list for two years. In 1952, Norman Vincent Peale—perhaps another forefather of New Age—brought us Power of Positive Thinking.[7] Think and Grow Rich[8] by Napoleon Hill was published in 1960 and is still one of my favorites.

The New Age may actually have begun earlier, even before the time of the U.S. Constitution. American statesmen John Adams, Thomas Jefferson, Benjamin Franklin, and others were members of a secret spiritual society called the Freemasons. They believed there was an esoteric truth underlining all religion and science. They met in secret for fear that members of other churches might persecute them. The Freemasons society was based on a belief in God and in the importance of charity and brotherly love. When they wrote the Declaration of Independence they declared "all men are created equal" and "one nation under God, with liberty and justice for all." With their faith in God, their vision of the future, were these also early visionaries of a New Age?

Figure 1: Many of our early forefathers were Freemasons. These are some of their symbols that appear on our one-dollar bill. The Egyptian pyramid represents a temple for spiritual initiation. The top of the pyramid is separate from the bottom, suggesting that the spirit is above the earth. From here the all-seeing eye, or Eye of Providence, watches. The eye is also seen within some divine rays, which represents the glory of God. The words ANNUIT CŒPTIS at the top mean "God has favored our undertakings." NOVUS ORDO SECLORUM at the bottom means "new order of the ages." Also (not shown), are the words IN GOD WE TRUST and E PURIBUS UNUM, which means "out of many, one."

Cosmology

According to the Hindus the world goes through a slow, continuous evolutionary cycle. This particular cycle is made up of four world periods, called yugas. Each yuga is thousands of years long. Through these long evolutionary periods we gradually evolve from a less spiritually developed state to an increasingly higher one. When the world reaches a pinnacle, it then eventually declines again, like the rise and fall of an empire. This cycle continues through the eons, over and over again. This process allows some souls to move along and others to move up to a higher heavenly existence. Things go from better to worse, and then eventually worse to better. Most Hindus believe our present age is the Kali Yuga, which is the lowest point in our spiritual development (see page 16). Others believe we have already passed through Kali Yuga, and have begun our slow ascent toward a higher spiritual state.

Apocalypse

In many of the most famous prophecies of the world, such as those in the Bible, of Nostradamus, Edgar Cayce, and others, there are predictions of an apocalypse, or period of mass destruction. Some have predicted this earthly hell may begin sometime between 1999 and 2012 A.D. Some Christians insist the end begins in 2021, and that Jesus is on his way back to save them. Many say this calamity is necessary to uproot the evil that now exists in the world. Regardless of what will actually happen, these predictions are motivating many people to come to terms with their own spiritual understanding.

The scriptures suggest this low period will result in an increased amount of greed. According to the scriptures, during this Kali Yuga period, many people will lack integrity. Unfortunately, this greed can also lead us to tamper with Mother Nature. According to the Hindus, this yuga must occur before the "Golden Age," or the Satya Yuga, can come about. The Golden Age is a time of spiritual renewal, when an awakening of consciousness will again bring a greater virtue and peace on earth. Doesn't this sound similar to the coming of the kingdom of heaven predicted in the Bible?

End of the World

I believe the end of our world is an experience each of us will face sometime during one of our lives—but not necessarily all of us at the same time. Perhaps the end refers to a catastrophic situation in one of our lifetimes, which suddenly changes or ends life as we know it. This event could cause us to unexpectedly lose everything. If we die, we may be sent to the spirit world without time to prepare. The scriptures tell us this doom may come about by a natural disaster; such as an earthquake, or by war, starvation, or an epidemic. We are warned we should get our spiritual life in order because we never know when we may meet with such an unexpected end.

Just as in the Bible, various cultures have also had their own doomsday predictions. Were these just specific predictions for each of these cultures? Can we assume these prophecies refer to the whole world at the same time? For example, in biblical times, people didn't even know that North America existed or that the earth was round. Perhaps many of their predictions refer only to the world as they knew it. In the Bible, the Jewish prophets foretell their people should expect a gruesome time in the future. These prophets predicted this would bring about a near complete destruction of their people. Is it possible Nazi Germany was the event Jewish prophets predicted a thousand years earlier?

Mayan

While I was in Mexico I met a Mayan guide who said his Mayan forefathers predicted the end of the world would come in 2011 A.D. He went on to say he had noticed the numbers of his people were declining more and more every year. They were being pushed further and further from their homeland and into more uninhabitable places. He said that before long, he felt the only real evidence of his ancient culture would be historical artifacts. I couldn't help wonder if the Mayans were predicting the end of their own civilization in 2011 but not necessarily the entire human race. Very little happens everywhere to everyone at the same time. While one country is experiencing floods, another may be having below average rainfall. While one nation is at war, others are experiencing peaceful times. Even the sun doesn't shine everywhere at the same time.

Astrology

The last two millenniums are referred to as the Age of Pisces. In astrology, in the precession of the equinoxes, it takes about twenty-four thousand years for the sun to wobble through all twelve astrological signs. According to astrology, the present age is in the sign of the vernal equinox. The autumnal equinox is now in Virgo, therefore we say that we are in the Age of Pisces. Pisces, among other things, is an Age of imagination and belief, which is a beautiful and fascinating thing. It has given rise to storytelling, devotion, sculpture, stage, music, motion pictures, and dance, all of which have flourished.

At the same time, people are also apt to believe what is untrue and act wrongly. For example, the age of Pisces began around the time of Christ, when people were persecuted for their faith. People like Jesus were actually tortured for their beliefs. It is ironic that many have been persecuted for both belief and nonbelief in Jesus. For it has also been through both belief in, and denial of Jesus that many have found salvation.

Pisces is the symbol of the two fish swimming in opposite directions. The fish, which represent the duality of our nature, live in water, which here represents the spirit. Pisces is the duality of our psychospiritual nature.

Many of the old prophecies have occurred during this Piscean Age, and this has led many to believe we are actually still seeing apocalyptic times now in certain parts of the world. Although not everything has happened everywhere at once, many predictions have come true in many countries in a relatively short time. There have been earthquakes, wars, starvation, pestilence (epidemics), revolts, droughts, floods, and even antichrists. There have been those religious leaders who have even led their followers to suicide. According to the predictions of the Kali Yuga, during this age, greed and materialism are said to often be irresistible temptations.

No one seems to disagree about the fact we are now in the Age of Pisces, but there is considerable debate as to when the next age, that of Aquarius begins. Some say it begins in 2012, others say 2100. According to others we are currently in a twenty-one-year transition period between the Ages, which goes from 1991 to 2012.[9] When the Aquarian Age does begin, astrology tells us that we can expect a time when humans will make great leaps and discoveries. Aquarius is the age of knowledge and the sign of humanity. We should continue to see a further blending of traditions, and a greater emphasis on knowledge, freedom, and equal rights.

In the coming Aquarian Age, worldwide trade is sure to be a major issue as natural resources continue to become scarcer. The planet Uranus rules Aquarius, and we should see a continuing emphasis on technology, communications, special effects, graphics, and electronics. Astrology tells us we can expect to see even greater marvels in technology during this age. The challenge will be not to lose touch with our heart and soul.

Alien Technology

Once I was at a large New Age exhibit and I saw a man looking with great admiration at an artist's model of a UFO. The gentleman commented to me that "based on the aerodynamics of a UFO, it was clear the aliens were much more spiritually advanced than we are." I wondered what he was seeing because all I was picking up on was the technology involved. Is a flying saucer more spiritual than an airplane? It is like saying a computer is more spiritual than a typewriter. Doesn't it depend on the intentions of the life form operating it? How conscious is this being and does it love other beings—even beings different from itself? We must ask ourselves if we are loving and compassionate. What is our own experience of consciousness? There is every extreme in existence, like love and hate, kind and unkind, and every shade between. The important point the Hindus make is that atoms in any form are still atoms—regardless of whether they are in the form of a spaceship or a large rock. Our spiritual existence is not made of atoms; it is made of emotions, conception, intuition, and knowledge.

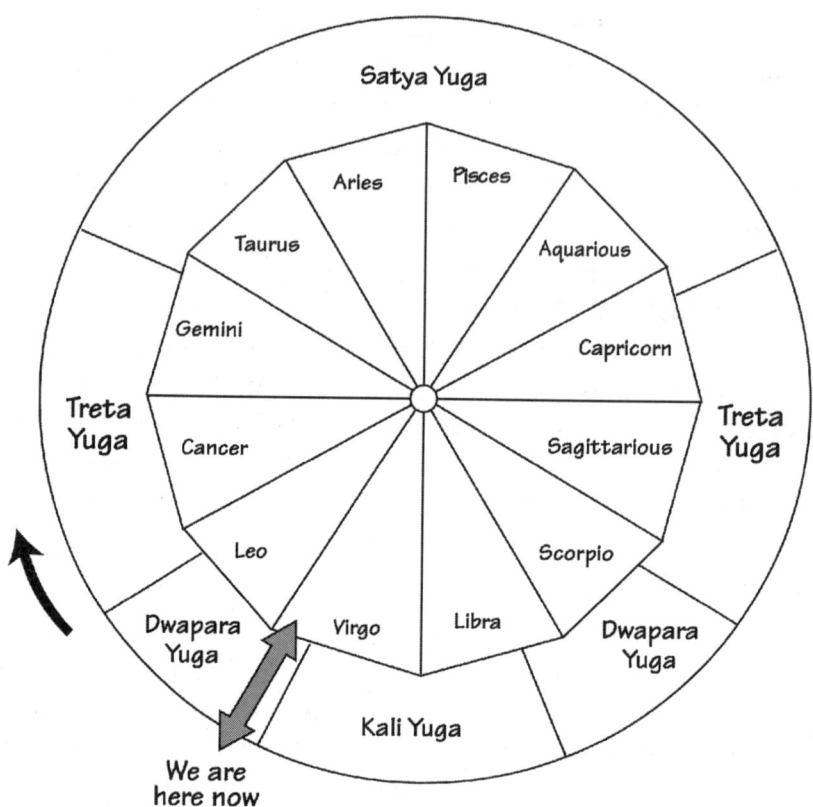

Figure 2: This diagram was adapted from a design by Swami Sri Yukteswarji. It shows the correlation between the Hindu yugas and the astrological precession of the equinoxes. Swami Yukteswarji speculated that we are now in the Dwapara Yuga (indicated by the location of the arrow) and that we entered this yuga in 1700 A.D. He suggests we will not enter the Aquarian Age until 2499 A.D. We travel clockwise from the Kali Yuga (which lasts for 2,400 years)—to the Dwapara Yuga (2,400 years)—to the Treta Yuga (3,600 years)—to the Satya Yuga (9,600 years)—and then around the other side through all the yugas again, and this cycle goes on over and over through the ages.

This is unlike other Hindus who say we are still in the Kali Yuga for another 426,898 years and that the Age of Aquarius begins around the year 2012 A.D. According to some of these sources,[10] the Kali Yuga began at midnight on February 18, 3102 B.C., which is also the year the Hindu calendar begins.

Freedom

When we think freedom means getting what we want, we're not seeing life through the eyes of our spirit. I am free when I am free of myself. Freedom is when we step outside of our thoughts, and see with clear amazement this world around us. When we feel a sense of wide-eyed wonder at this miracle we call life, then we are truly free. To our spirit, there is nothing that isn't already a part of ourselves. Our spirit is the moment. It needs nothing and it accepts every moment. We can laugh or cry or help in what's going on or not—it's up to us. In this state we see our spirit is always aware, but our memories and perceptions often preoccupy our mind. The subjectivity driven by our ego is what clouds our perceptions.

For example, my hand is free as long as I'm not holding on to anything, right? My hand can be free one moment and hanging on the next. I can be holding on to something and not mentally holding on at the same time. My hand might be holding on, but my mind isn't. In other words, I can let my hand hold on, while at the same time my mind isn't if I am not my hand. This awareness that "I'm not my hand," but instead "I am the one with a hand" is known as Karma Yoga. From this vantage point you see you have an ego that acts through the body, but you are not just your body or your ego. We are actually the thought behind our body and soul. We are the awareness beyond ourselves.

The scriptures say our body actually materializes from thought. And you begin to see everything in your life is just a spirit. Even a baby's pacifier is a spirit. Your car, a telephone are consciousness in a play. When we let go of our bias, we have the presence of mind of this much larger perspective. An obvious example of Karma Yoga in action is seen in the life of people such as Jesus Christ, Mother Teresa, or Mahatma Gandhi. This is what is meant by being a Karma Yogi.

Liberation

"It is harder for a rich man to get into the kingdom of heaven than it is for a camel to pass through the eye of a needle."[11]

There has also been a long-standing tradition in both the East and West that requires priests to forsake a worldly life. The ancient scriptures suggest that unless we resist a craving for things, we are not likely to find our way to heaven. They believe that in order to achieve salvation, we must let go of any selfish interest and devote oneself to a spiritual life. Then we experience more of ourselves, spiritually speaking. When a total loss of identity occurs, we realize we are not our body but a spirit. We see we are not really our name, age, sex, nationality, or religion. Through this process of illumination we begin to peel off one layer at a time. Like peeling back the layers of an onion, we discover there is nothing left inside and yet everything is left. The Eastern Scriptures tell us the secret is when you are not merely a thing, you are everything. Because everything comes from one and when you are not separate you are one. Some who have experienced this in a past life may quickly recall this experience during meditation or hypnosis.

The previous quote comparing the rich man to a camel seems to be about our struggle for self-realization. Is it any wonder many seekers in this Piscean Age choose to forgo self-inquiry? Many are willing to simply accept the conclusions of the ancient sages "that all is God, and I am that." The scriptures warn us, however, if we accept this truth about our ultimate divinity, without actually transcending our ego, we will run the risk of using this truth to convince ourselves of something we want to believe. When we are thinking too frequently about what we want, we miss the collective aspect of our lives. Then we are liable to do unfair things to others. We may say it is because "others get away with doing something, why not me?"

Astrology predicts that during the time of the Picean Age, life will have developed many challenges for us. These challenges can often overshadow a quest for self-understanding. It seems our attention is constantly being diverted. We see extreme examples of this love and hate, in people like Mother Teresa to rulers like Hitler. There have been those during this age who have opened their hearts and minds and have shown tremendous compassion for others. While others who have murdered rationalize it by saying "if I am a God, then what I want must be destiny."

Self-Surrender

In Mark 8:34, Jesus spoke of a surrendering to the kingdom of heaven. He said, "If anyone would come after me, he must deny himself and take up his cross and follow me." It appears Jesus is saying that if one wishes to find truth in heaven, one must transcend oneself in this struggle for freedom. This invitation is not always appropriate for some people and not desirable to many who still wish in some way to better themselves. I have noticed in my meditation classes that some people are interested in gaining self-knowledge and approach meditation as a form of self-exploration. For others, meditation is a way to experience greater relaxation and to help them to get more of what they want in life.

Through our spiritual consciousness we can have a deep intuitive understanding that we are all truly the same. Our spiritual self, or soul, can experience existence as part of a unified whole. It sees that we are all God's children, and it doesn't matter if we are rich or poor, educated or uneducated, black, white, or brown. Those who have experienced this say that in their daily lives they begin to feel like they are just watching themselves. They see that their actions are more a process of their mind and body just acting in accordance with its programming. These people observe themselves playing their part in the world—whatever that happens to be. They see that they exist, and that they are the one observing themselves at the same time. They have the feeling that they are "in this world, but not of this world." Eventually they begin to sense the presence of God everywhere. Eastern yoga calls this experience Karma Yoga.

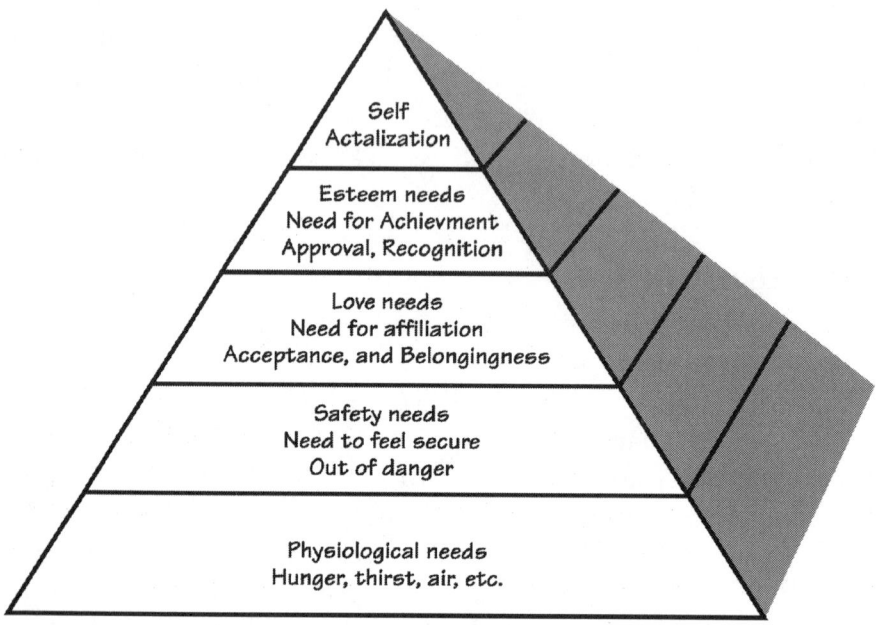

Figure 3: Data on "Hierarchy of Needs" from Motivation and Personality by A. H. Maslow (Harper and Row, 1954).

Psychologist Dr. Abraham Maslow presented an example of the ascending order of human needs. Maslow arranged motives and needs according to an order of hierarchy, from the more basic frequent needs to the higher aesthetic ones.

The basic needs, such as hunger and safety, must be met first or this will tend to dominate a person's attention. If you are hungry, for example, you will continue to search for food until you are satisfied. If this need and other safety needs are met, then love is what you will probably seek next. If love goes unfulfilled, the pursuit of love may be all this person has time for and the self-actualizing needs may not be very significant. If the satisfaction of love is fulfilled, then aesthetic needs will be very important to the individual. Maslow reasoned that a person's aesthetic and spiritual needs can best be served when their other needs are no longer an issue.

Material Success

According to many in this New Age, being financially successful is not necessarily contrary to living a spiritual life! Many say, if our spiritual life comes first, we can learn to manage a material life and make the right choices. From a spiritual point of view, the question is, have we learned to truly see and appreciate others? In fact, it might very well be that future success comes to us from an ability to serve other people's needs. From a material point of view, many people will succeed if they can truly satisfy one or more of our needs. Psychologists suggest that besides a need for short- and long-term survival (food, shelter, protection, and security), we have a need to feel important. We also have a need for sexual gratification, a sense of belongingness, and to be loved and to love others. Satisfying these needs is what provides us with the challenges in our life. We grow by overcoming these challenges.

Many very successful people are considered also among some of the most enlightened. They're finding success in the center of a growing spiritual awakening, and an emerging universal consciousness. Maslow suggests a quest for self-actualization reins highest, and eventually this is what will bring us true spiritual fulfillment.

The Upanishads

The ancient Indian Upanishads tell us that our relationship with the material things of this world is balanced when we are neither running away from nor desperately chasing after anything, when we are neither hoarding wealth nor squandering it. Some people, however, tend to be preoccupied with their own material advantage, while others may feel they must always be self-sacrificing to be spiritual. Some people swing between these extremes, and some lean more one way or the other. Yet others find a balance between their needs and the needs of others. Since we are both body and spirit, the scriptures remind us we cannot ignore either. In truth, we are neither above nor below anyone. Our needs are neither more nor less important than anyone else's. The important question is, have we learned to really love others, life, and ourselves? Have we learned these things are important spiritually?

Destiny

Each of us is unique, and yet, an essential part of the whole. Each of us makes our own contribution to this planet and to each other. We each have a particular part we can play in this world and something we can offer. Our fate, or destiny, is known as our dharma in Eastern religion. We each have the potential to manifest love and to develop a talent or interest in something. Based on our own individual experiences, we can give our own personal service to the planet and its inhabitants. When we are not in touch with ourselves, or perhaps not aware of our own significance, this is when we may find ourselves feeling lost and simply doing what we see others do or what they tell us. The scriptures, however, remind us our greatest fulfillment comes when we feel God's presence in our life and we engage in something that allows us to be ourselves while serving others at the same time.

Our primary challenge is to transcend ourselves and to understand what our motives and intentions are. We must let go of any bias or prejudices and unlearn all of our negative ways of thinking. We need to discover through quiet contemplation the soul's spirit that lies within us. Then we start to feel we are not here by accident and that we are fulfilling a certain need of existence. It is up to us to know ourselves and to learn who we are, while also remembering to appreciate others. Everyone craves attention and wants to feel important. With so many people all trying to get attention at the same time, is it any wonder so many people feel unfulfilled? The scriptures say God can work through each of us, to spread love to others.

In God's Service

Our part in all this is to explore what we have an interest in doing and learn how to best do it. Each of us must make our own way in this world, and we need to discover how we can best put ourselves to use. Since you cannot separate your work from your life, or your life from who you are, through our work we can express our love and devotion to God and to one another. When we ask God to work through our lives, the Holy Spirit guides us if we will just listen and give ourselves to God's service. The scriptures say we will be guided to what we need to do to fulfill our destiny.

God knows how each of us can best put our gifts to use. Being in God's service does not mean being helpless or poor. Imagine if you were in the service of a king. The king is the ruler of his entire kingdom and you are going about the king's business. Whatever resources you would need to complete your mission would be granted to you by way of the king. God is behind us when we are living our dharma, but we can only discover God deep within our own hearts.

Opening Doors of Perception

In this past millennium, religious teachings have been revised to stay current with science and the social issues of today. For example, years ago when science said the earth was not the center of our solar system, certain people denied this because it contradicted their present teachings. At the time they insisted the earth *was* at the center. Today, however, all religions know this is not true in light of a preponderance of new scientific evidence. Other such scientific knowledge is, however, still being denied, and many of us today are left asking ourselves what we really believe.

Two studies that have contributed greatly to the development of our modern consciousness are the philosophies of Zen and Neuro-Linguistics. Both of these suggest that as long as we experience a world through our senses, we're always gathering our impressions from a very small fraction of the information available around us. And it is through this subjective lens that we get our impressions of what the world is. Since perceptions vary and are vast and incomplete, our brain filters reality so we can get a "sense" of what is going on, otherwise we would be in a trance and overwhelmed. This process allows us to be a part of the whole and yet the whole at the same time. The body and the brain are like the hardware of a computer, and life is like being on-line. Your mind is like the software. The software of our mind and senses allows us to manage this vast information.

The heart of the Internet is the soul and spirit of its users. And, you can experience all sorts of programs, information, viruses, perspectives, and viewpoints.

Once I spoke with Krishnamurti, and I sensed it was through this very heightened awareness that he could see the world. It amazed me; I wondered how it was he could see so much more. It seemed he was aware of even some of the most subtle influences motivating me and affecting my behavior. He was aware of so many of the things that were so important to those who came to see him. Often, it seemed like it was the things we may have taken for granted. He urged us to just look and observe these things for ourselves.

Of the 15 billion neurons in our brain, the vast majority of the feelings and thoughts we experience are not even on a conscious level. We are, however, assimilating enormous amounts of data on an unconscious level, and this greatly influences us. As humans we have emotions, intuition, and empathy, in addition to the factuality of the intellect. It is through our hearts and minds we experience God. When you have a pure, loving heart, you have gone beyond witnessing to being. The great yogis who have seen God are overwhelmed. All they can finally say is, "All is one!" If we were equipped with only an intellectual understanding, we would be like Mr. Spock in *Star Trek*. With only logic and objectivity we would miss out on the spiritual reality and love.

Zen

Zen is a very effective philosophy for melting away our prejudices. It originated in Japan in about 520 A.D. by a man from Ceylon, named Bodhidharma. For nine years Bodhidharma contemplated in the mountains, and he emerged a great being. His message was to encourage us to transcend and expand beyond our individual viewpoints, which eventually allows us to perceive existence itself. Existence, according to Bodhidharma, is something that only happens spontaneously. All of this life we perceive is constantly in a state of motion, vibrating at a certain frequency. Every atom in the universe is somewhere slightly different every millionth of a second.

What, then, is existence? Zen says that existence is instantaneous. Since the earth is constantly moving, and our thoughts and bodies are constantly in a state of flux, what we really *are* can only be experienced in each moment. For example, what is a cloud? Is the cloud what it was a second ago, or what it has changed into in the next moment? In fact, the moment I say the word "cloud," no sooner than the word comes out of my mouth the cloud has changed slightly.

In fact, anything that can be explained, according to Zen, must be in the past tense. Even if it's about my most immediate feelings and thoughts, it is not the same exact experience the second after it passes through my mind. I might think of fear, but is my experience of this fear exactly the same, even a second later? NLP researchers estimate our minds perceive about 12,000 separate impressions every second. This is in terms of everything we see, hear, smell, taste, and feel. And these are only the impressions that are operating at this certain frequency. This doesn't even include radio waves, X-rays, microwaves, and millions of other vibrations outside this range.

What *is* reality then? Isn't it always a very spontaneous experience of existence? Are any of my opinions actually true in the absolute sense of the word? Can we know what is the absolute perspective? Aren't my perceptions my own individual experience of what I perceive? For example, people thought for centuries that the sun moved through their sky and that the earth was stationary. This might have been true for these people at that time, but how true is it from an absolute perspective of the universe? Can we even know what is the absolute perspective?

Through our minds, there are a number of viewpoints possible at each moment, and collectively, there are an infinite number of possibilities. Consequently, there are an infinite number of realities, and in any absolute sense, existence itself is inexpressible. How can we actually experience existence then?

From a Zen perspective the question is why do we not experience it? Zen says that if we are not busy entertaining a personal version of what we think existence is—in other words, if we are not assuming an interpretation of what existence is, at that moment—we will experience existence instantaneously, spontaneously. Zen says when we don't experience existence, it's because we are involved in a certain play, or reality. If we let go and don't create existence, then existence simply *is*. This is what Zen calls the *transcendental world*. Normally, we are encouraged to create a certain existence—often like somebody else, or what NLP calls a model of the world. However, according to NLP, this model is like a photograph, frozen in time.

Zen says to simply *look*. For example, imagine if a video camera followed you around everywhere you went. Watching this movie would be funny, boring, interesting, and embarrassing, and you would see you're not always acting the way you thought you were. Sometimes, we may be acting better than we think. This sort of movie is all we would need to gain tremendous self-understanding. To witness ourselves and to step back and just see like the camera provides an extraordinary glimpse of our reality.

Zen consists of two different schools: Soto Zen and Rinzai. Both emphasize the importance of this witnessing. Soto Zen underscores that through regular practice of meditation, or "serene reflection," you become more aware of the way things are. Gradually through this reflection, you can see many things more clearly.

Have you ever gone to a group meeting or a class where you have no idea of what's going on? It's easy to sit back and just watch, isn't it? When you are impartial and not attached to any particular viewpoint, you can simply observe. You can see how the various people in the scene are; who the authority figures; the planners, doubters, builders, and who the hard workers are. When you're witnessing, you see things from different perspectives.

But things quickly change when we have a vested interest in something. Suppose you are attending a meeting to "save the whales," something you feel very passionate about. In this situation, it will probably become much harder for you to be accepting of an opposing viewpoint. You may tend to take what is said more personally, and it may be harder for you to be relaxed and accepting. In Hinduism, these are called *vasanas*, which are those subliminal traits that shape our attitude and opinions. Zen says, Just Look! Drop the opinions.

Meditation

For thousands of years the question has been, how can our mind become spontaneous and yet aware? The key, Zen says, is found in meditation. In Zen, meditation is witnessing, and "emptying the mind" (see pages 38 to 39). With just a momentary experience of this spacious awareness, our mind is free. And, if only for a few moments, it allows us to experience a transcendental awareness. Then we see we are free to choose the battles we want and responsible to know which ones count and which don't. Have you ever noticed how many disagreements are over trivial things? It is usually when our feelings are hurt that we will argue over almost anything. Wars and feuds have been started over simple disagreements.

Each interpretation of the world we have may either support or conflict with the rest of our interpretations. It is how these interpretations fit together that determine our psychological well-being. When we have inner conflict and there is a disagreement going on inside, this is what NLP calls an incongruency—and this is what is responsible for our mental, emotional, and physical problems. Zen says it can dissolve these incongruencies and bring about a freedom from our own thinking. Through Zen, you realize no opinion has any real hold over you, other than that which you imagine. You see thoughts as useful, or not; it all depends on what you want and who you are. You see that integrity and compassion are what bring peace.

Rinzai

In Rinzai, besides silent meditation one cultivates a free awareness through contemplating certain paradoxical sentences, known as *koans*. An example of a koan is, "Once a Zen teacher clapped his hands and asked, 'What is the sound of one hand clapping?'" Through meditating on such statements, which defy logic, students may find one day they suddenly let go of their reasoning. (In Buddhism this is called "no mind.") Without desire, the pupil has an actual experience of an instantaneous existence. Unanticipated, the person may experience *nirvana*. This state, the Buddhists say, is beyond thought, words, form, or description. This is what Zen calls the experience of enlightenment. In yoga this state is called *Nirvikalpa Samadhi*, or God realization. Usually, however, our teachers, parents, and peers want us to agree with them. They are looking for a certain predetermined answer from us. We look for these answers in the contents of our past and what others have told us. "Where is that answer? I know it's in there somewhere."

In school, we are required to memorize dates, certain answers, established concepts, which we must later recall in order to pass our examinations. You can read many books full of information and not learn to step outside your own pattern of thinking to clearly see and observe.

In the East, when one speaks of a God-realized person, one is referring to an individual who has experienced liberation and gone beyond the ego. This person has let go of his or her identity, so that they simply exist in the moment. All who have experienced this say, "All is one, and one is all." At such moments, these people are no longer who they thought they were. The Indian saint Ramakrishna once spoke about this state. Like Krishnamurti, he saw we only need to let go of an illusion of separateness, created by our ego, to experience oneness. Ramakrishna once said:

> "In that state a man no longer feels the existence of his ego. And who is there left to seek it? Who can describe

how he feels in that state—in his own Pure Consciousness—about the real nature of God? There is a sign of Perfect Knowledge. A man becomes silent when it is attained. . . . As long as his self-analysis is not complete, a man argues with much ado. But he becomes silent when he completes it. When the empty pitcher has been filled with water, when the water inside the pitcher becomes one with the water of the lake outside, no more sound is heard. . . . All trouble and botheration come to an end when the 'I' dies. You may indulge in thousands of reasonings, but still the 'I' doesn't disappear. For people like you and me it is good to have the feeling, 'I am a lover of God'." [12]

The Art of Meditation

Ancient scriptures have proclaimed meditation nothing short of a direct means to enlightenment. Many New Age books have claimed it to be a remedy for everything from cancer to self-doubt to a host of other things. What do the Eastern scriptures tell us about meditation? We're going to start with the remedy aspect, then we'll get deeper into the spiritual aspects of meditation.

What if by using a very simple technique for just a few minutes a day you could substantially reduce the amount of stress in your life, have a more cheerful outlook, increase your body's immune system, add years to your life, understand yourself better, and attain an inner peace that would see you through life's most difficult times? Would you do it? If your answer is *yes*, meditation might be just the thing for you!

Meditation is simply a natural way of quieting the mind and experiencing an inner sense of peace. It is allowing ourselves a quiet, calm state, just below our thoughts. For example, think of a lake that is completely calm and still. Imagine there are no ripples on the surface and the water reflects a very clear image of its surroundings. You can see everything beautifully—the trees along the shore, the rolling hills, mountains, the blue sky, and clouds. However, if a stone drops into the water it raises waves.

These waves disrupt the reflection, and you can no longer see as clearly.

The mind is like this lake, and our thoughts are like the ripples on its surface. When our brain waves are measured, they actually appear like waves with peaks and valleys. The lower the rate, the calmer and more serene the mind is. Perhaps you can remember moments of serenity, such as sitting outside on an incredibly clear night and gazing at the stars. Imagine, the immensity of space and the galaxies. Try staring into the heavens on a clear, dark night. Look at the millions of stars and you can feel yourself transcending your earthly concerns. Day-to-day problems have a way of diminishing in the face of this vastness. Or maybe sitting on the beach at sunset beneath a breathtaking sky. Your mind may at these moments become calm, quiet, and still. This is the quiet reflective state called meditation. It is at moments such as these you feel a sense of tranquility, where everything seems to be just right. You may have experienced this while sitting quietly and listening to the rain, or watching the flames inside a fireplace. When people say, "I need to take time to smell the roses," what they also mean is, "I need to take time to meditate." You may have also taken a break by walking through a park, and if this has helped to calm and clear your mind, this too was meditation.

Meditation One

To start

Find a quiet place where you can be comfortable, either sitting or lying down. Loosen any tight clothing. Sit on the floor in a cross-legged position, on a cushion or pillow. Sitting upright will keep you awake. Keep your back, neck, and head in a straight vertical line. Imagine that you are a marionette and a string is attached to the top of your head pulling up, keeping everything in a straight line. This allows your bones and muscles to be free from tension. It also allows nerve energy to flow smoothly. If you are slumped over or your back is bent, you tend to build up tension in your shoulders and neck. There are various cross-legged

The Art of Meditation

positions that are also very effective in keeping the spine straight, but they can often be difficult to maintain unless you are very limber. If you sit in a simple cross-legged position on the floor, try sitting on a pillow or cushion and this will eliminate the tendency to fall back or slump forward.

Place your hands comfortably on your lap or on your thighs. Keep a couple fingers touching together or allow your hands to just rest inside one another. If you don't want to sit in this upright position because of a back or health problem, then perhaps a reclining chair would be more appropriate. If there isn't one, then you can even lie on a bed or on the floor, with a low pillow or blanket under your head. If you lie down and you're feeling as if you might fall asleep, you can prop one arm up, so if you begin to go to sleep you will awaken yourself as your arm begins to drop. If you have a limited amount of time, position a clock were you can peek at it now and then. Avoid setting an alarm clock as it can be too jarring when it goes off. Also, allow at least one hour after a meal before meditating.

Once you're ready

Start by stretching. Stretch your legs, neck, arms, and back. Then pick a spot to settle into and start breathing deeply and slowly through your nose for a couple of minutes. Breathe deeply so the air goes all the way down into your belly. If you're unsure if you are breathing into the belly, just place one hand on your belly and notice if your hand is rising and falling. Get into a nice rhythm and feel the continuous flow of your breath. One secret to breathing deeply this way is to push your breath just a bit further when you breathe out. With your next breath, you'll breathe more deeply, filling more of your lungs.

Continue to breathe deeply and steadily for a couple of minutes; concentrate only on the rise and fall of your breathing. After a couple of minutes, allow your breathing to be more natural and comfortable. Then gently shift your attention to your nostrils. Continue to breathe naturally, focusing on your nose. Notice how the air is slightly cooler inside as you inhale, slightly warmer as you exhale. When you feel your thoughts drifting onto something else, let it happen. Allow your attention to go wherever it goes. When you see what is there, just watch. Whatever happens in your thoughts, imagine you are looking at a screen in your mind's eye, like watching a movie . When your attention is free again, go back to your breathing. That's all there is to it!

This form of meditation is called *mindfulness*. It is a process of simply watching your thoughts. It's not *what* you're thinking that is important but that you are watching your thoughts rather than being wrapped up in them. In this type of meditation you don't identify with anything or get lost in what comes up. You simply watch things happen. This witnessing is the meditation. Nothing is considered a distraction. Go with whatever thoughts, feelings, or sensations come up. Imagine you are witnessing something is happening to someone else.

At first, it may be difficult to sit like this for very long. You may feel restless, and your mind may wander a lot. Pick an amount of time comfortable for you—even if it is just a few minutes a day. For the first couple of months meditate every day—twice a day, if possible. This way, you will develop a habit of meditating. In the beginning it is better to meditate for less time but to do it consistently, than for longer periods sporadically. Gradually, increase your time to allow twenty minutes, morning and evening. For example, if you only meditate for ten minutes the first two days, increase your time to eleven or twelve minutes by the third day. Be consistent, and don't allow yourself excuses. If you say to yourself, "I'll skip today and do twice as much time tomorrow," you may end up owing yourself a lot of time by the end of the week.

Other helpful hints

Morning and evening are usually ideal times to meditate, but pick a time of day when your body feels like relaxing and when you are in a comfortable setting where you won't be disturbed. You may want to turn off the ringer on your telephone or pager. If possible arrange the same time and place to meditate each day and make sure the environment is free of distractions. If you have young children you can tie a handkerchief around your door knob to indicate when you are meditating or, you may want to meditate while they are asleep or taking a nap. It is ideal if you can have a separate room or dedicate a corner of a room for your meditation. Subdued lighting, fresh air, candles, flowers, and incense can help create the right mood.

Include in your meditation place any spiritual articles—a picture of Jesus, a cross, a statue of Buddha, or whatever helps you bring about a spiritual feeling. Some people also enjoy singing, chanting, or playing a musical instrument. Some prefer silence, and others like soft music or environmental sounds such as the ocean, a running stream, or a rainstorm can also be helpful. Meditation is not a state in which we are "wrapped up in our thoughts." In meditation, your thoughts seem to be unraveling. If questions come up, let them remain unanswered unless answers simply reveal themselves. Make an initial commitment to practice meditation twice a day, for at least five to twenty minutes. Be sure to give yourself plenty of time to adjust to the practice of meditation. In gradual steps over a three-week period, you can increase your meditation time slowly.

At the end of this chapter there is a chart to help you keep track of your meditations (see page 44).

Meditation Two

In all meditations you start by concentrating on something so that other thoughts begin to fade. In the previous meditation, it was your breath. For this exercise, you may focus on anything—the sound of the wind, rain, or ocean. You can also repeat a sentence, or *mantra*, over and over again. Some people have used mantras such as, "God is love, love one another," or "Jesus Christ, come to my aid." By simply repeating a phrase, you eventually become absorbed into it and you eventually lose all other train of thought. When you repeat something over and over, its sound vibration and intention can also transform you. If you repeat the name of "God," for instance, it can actually draw you closer to God. In the East, this is what is called the practice of *bhakti*, or devotion. You actually experience the ideal and lose all sense of time and limitation through prayer, singing, and dancing.

You can meditate with your eyes open or closed. If you would rather have your eyes open, try this simple meditation: Place a lit candle or light bulb on a table a foot or two away. Sit straight up and adjust the light to slightly above your eye level. Stare at the flame or light. Each time your attention drifts to something else, observe what's there, then gently guide your attention back to the light. In this way, other thoughts will slowly begin to fade and become unimportant. Eventually, you can lose all sense of time and place. At this point, your mind can experience reflection, like that of a calm and tranquil lake.

Meditation Three

If your mind seems particularly active, try this great "breath-counting" meditation. After you have done a couple minutes of slow deep breathing, start counting your breaths from one to four. Once you reach four, start over without pausing. Each time you exhale, count the next number, and then when you inhale say "and" with each inhalation. As you exhale, begin by saying "one," and then as you inhale say "and," going all the way up to "four." When you get to four, start right over again without pausing.

For example, exhale as you say "one…(inhale) and…(exhale) two…(inhale) and…(exhale) three…(inhale) and…(exhale) four…(inhale) and…(exhale) one…(inhale) and…(exhale) two…(inhale) and…(exhale) three…," and so on. Just keep starting over at four, counting over and over again without pausing.

At first, you might lose track of counting as your mind wanders and you forget what number you are on. Or you might count out of sequence. Don't worry about it—just gently guide your attention back to the counting. The important thing isn't how accurately you perform the counting, it's how relaxed your mind becomes.

Continue counting for several minutes or until you feel completely relaxed. Usually in Zen meditation, you count from one to ten. I prefer one to four to start with because the faster turn-around time does not give your mind much chance to wander. Do this meditation once or twice a day and you can't help but go into a trance within just a few minutes. After a while, your counting becomes automatic and you won't even be thinking about it. It feels like there is a part of your mind that is experiencing a blissful inner state of awareness.

Naturally occurring states

Have you ever driven your car several blocks across town and you don't even remember driving? This is an example of a trance. Once I was walking along engrossed in thought and I looked up, and there was a huge bright sunflower hanging over a fence. It was so close to my face, it caught me by surprise, and I became mesmerized for a moment. I forgot where I was going and what I was supposed to be doing. This lasted for just a few moments, but it was a wonderful, blissful feeling. This is another example of a trance. Often, after a few weeks of meditating, you will begin to feel this sense of peace and tranquillity. With just a little practice each day, within a couple months you can experience a very alert, peaceful feeling. At first if you are feeling particularly restless, you can simply lie on the floor and listen to relaxing music for a while. This is an easy way to prepare yourself to learn meditation.

Restlessness

If you are like many people, you may have at least some initial resistance to meditation. You might even come up with all sorts of reasons why you can't meditate, such as "I have to clean the hall closet today," or "I have to sharpen the blades on the lawn mower." Our conscious mind may act like a child who doesn't want to go to bed. The mind can be afraid it will miss out on something or lose control. Have you ever noticed that at bedtime, children will suddenly need something out of nowhere, like a glass of milk? Children may be concerned that no matter how sleepy they are, they will miss out on something if they go to bed. You may also feel resistance because you think it is "lazy" to sit around and do nothing.

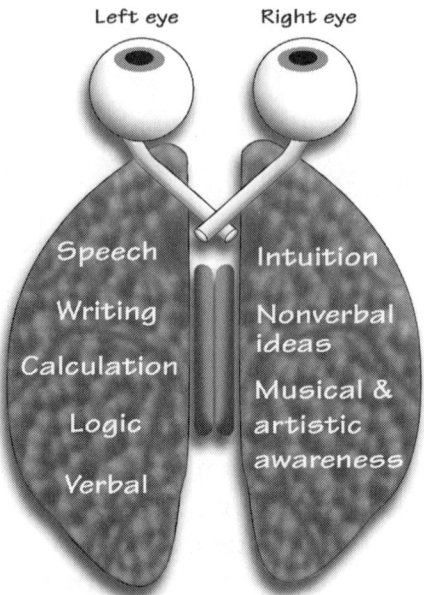

Figure 4: This schematized top view of the brain and eyes shows the different functions located on each side. The Human brain has a right and left half, or hemisphere. Certain learning and memory functions such as language, are located only in one hemisphere. Memories, however, are stored in vast patterns of interconnecting neurons, or *neural nets*, and each can be reached through many different pathways. Research has shown that greater communication between the two hemispheres of the brain, can be achieved by regular meditation. Meditation allows us to integrate these two halves.

Right hemisphere—controls the left side of the body, intuition, musical and artistic awareness.

Left hemisphere—controls the right side of the body, verbal activity, logic, sequential, and practical thinking.

The mind may also want to stay in control of what is allowed to become conscious. Sometimes while meditating, people may become aware of unconscious feelings. When the conscious mind lets go, sometimes what a person has been feeling inside may come up. If this happens, handle this the best you can. Sometimes you may allow yourself to feel whatever is there. Other days you may want to end your meditation early. Be understanding and take care of yourself the best you can. Be sure to get professional help if you need to. Meditation is often a subtle, gradual form of therapy. When things are going well, get in the habit of meditating at least once or twice a day. Half the battle is just getting yourself to sit down. Be sure to allow yourself a couple of minutes to slowly bring yourself out of meditation. Afterwards this will help you carry more of this state into the rest of your day. After a while it gets easier, and you will enjoy it more and more. Make it fun and pleasurable!

Religion and Meditation

Although you don't have to be a member of any particular religion to practice meditation, it has been a part of every religion. In the Bible, meditation is called *contemplation*. In Asian cultures, people have used meditation for centuries to better understand themselves and appreciate the true meaning of their lives. Native Americans called meditation a *vision quest*, or *perceiving quest*. In the United States, we have used such expressions as "I'm going to take a break," or "I need a moment to myself," to express this need for quiet reflection.

Since ancient times, meditators have also reported that besides initially relieving stress, meditation is a way to gain self-understanding. The beginning stages are similar to what was discussed in the previous chapter. In these stages, you experience a very clear intuition or a sense that you just simply know certain things without knowing how you know them. As this experience expands, you begin to feel you are more and more a witness to your life. This is the stage called *savikalpa* explained in the ancient science of Dhyana Yoga. Through the practice of this yoga, the consciousness of an individual expands until he or she experiences a state of cosmic synchronicity, called *samadhi*. There are several levels to this experience of oneness.

Eventually, we may no longer feel we are the leading character in our life, and we experience a sense of personal decentralization. We may feel like we are one of several characters in a play, and whatever is happening seems like it is happening to someone else. In psychology, the term for this state is *disassociation*. It is different if you become disassociated through meditation. When you experience this juxtaposition gradually through meditation, rather than from an illness or trauma, you remain aware in this state and you understand where you are and how you got there.

As samadhi continues, you begin to sense you are the same as everyone else. You see that you, your parents, and friends are all reflections of each other. As with a hall of mirrors at a carnival, you know the various reflections are you, although you look very different in each. To a naive observer, someone who is in samadhi can easily be thought of as insane or psychotic. That is why so many prophets were thought to be crazy. They see that whatever people do to others, they are actually doing to themselves at the same time. At this point, an ethical code is no longer needed to support this persons moral character. In samadhi, people see for themselves that they and others are actually the same. They see that it is when we forget this we experience a sense of separateness. As the old proverb reminds us, "Do unto others as you would have them do unto you."

Nirvikalpa Samadhi

Since existence manifests itself from a oneness, everything that exists is a result of a split in *that* one. The first split was into two. Then began an endless number of divisions, so mind-boggling one can't possibly comprehend all the divisions. From this first split came positive and negative, and then it went to quarters, but you don't lose the first two, so there are six, or three, or seven. Then the divisions continue endlessly, and yet they are all still one at the same time. As new divisions occur, nothing that ever is, or was, ever isn't. And, the variety is endless.

In nature, for example, at one point there are the elements, or the seasons, or the species, and all these things are interrelated. One system springs from another, with each pattern down the line still having an effect over the further divisions occurring within it. Everything is always relative to its preceding pattern, always evolving but neverending. So the one original source of the universe subdivides and becomes all the things that exist—and all things are also this one at the same time.

In the highest stages of samadhi, or Nirvikalpa Samadhi, the scriptures tell us we experience everything as an undifferentiated whole. One loses all sense of separateness and experiences the limitlessness of existence. In this state, no trace of the ego is left. In the Upanishads, Upadesaahasri says, "That wherein disappears the whole of that which affects the mind, and that which is also the background of all—to THAT I bow—the all eternal consciousness, the witness of all exhibitions of the Intellect."[13]

Oneness

In Islam the Sufis call this oneness *fana*. In Zen it is called *satori*. Jesus called this "the peace that passes all understanding." The Hopi Indians call it *Maasauu*, or *Great Spirit*. They all tell us this universal consciousness is the one source of all things. Jesus spoke of "my father who art in heaven." Jesus also taught that God is in each man. Our individual consciousness is only a small collection of thoughts of this limitless sea of consciousness. Our own mind is held together by only a thread of beliefs, values, and ideas. These are what supports our ego and sense of reality. We often hold tight to this reality, and our internal dialog distracts us from a more complete experience of existence. We are usually instructed to become something in particular. We lose our greater awareness because we get so wrapped up in our thoughts. Relaxation response, deep relaxation, and relaxation training are all forms of meditation.

In meditation, it is really in not being (who we think we are) that we experience what is beyond ourselves. It is in the absence of thought that we find this spacious awareness. When we are deep asleep, and even our dreams are quiet, our mind is immersed in peaceful silence. However, rarely are we awake for this experience. When we become aware of our thoughts melting into silence, this is meditation.

From these experiences come a new awareness, then gradually understanding. Buddha taught that if we could experience silence and become aware of our thoughts stopping—for even a split second—in that gap between our thoughts, we would experience the infinite or nirvana. Our own intuition is what is on the fringe of this silence, which is why we can often sense things more clearly than our mind can perceive. Through meditation you may feel a deep and profound sense of intuition, wellness, and joy. Enjoy!

Meditation Time Table

	\multicolumn{20}{c}{MINUTES IN MEDITATION PER SESSION}

	1	2	3	4	5	6	7	8	9	10	11	12	13	14	15	16	17	18	19	20
DAY 1					▓	▓	▓	▓	▓	▓	▓	▓	▓	▓	▓	▓	▓	▓	▓	▓
DAY 2						▓	▓	▓	▓	▓	▓	▓	▓	▓	▓	▓	▓	▓	▓	▓
DAY 3							▓	▓	▓	▓	▓	▓	▓	▓	▓	▓	▓	▓	▓	▓
DAY 4								▓	▓	▓	▓	▓	▓	▓	▓	▓	▓	▓	▓	▓
DAY 5									▓	▓	▓	▓	▓	▓	▓	▓	▓	▓	▓	▓
DAY 6										▓	▓	▓	▓	▓	▓	▓	▓	▓	▓	▓
DAY 7											▓	▓	▓	▓	▓	▓	▓	▓	▓	▓
DAY 8												▓	▓	▓	▓	▓	▓	▓	▓	▓
DAY 9													▓	▓	▓	▓	▓	▓	▓	▓
DAY 10														▓	▓	▓	▓	▓	▓	▓
DAY 11															▓	▓	▓	▓	▓	▓
DAY 12																▓	▓	▓	▓	▓
DAY 13																	▓	▓	▓	▓
DAY 14																		▓	▓	▓
DAY 15																			▓	▓
DAY 16																				▓
DAY 17																				
DAY 18																				
DAY 19																				
DAY 20																				
DAY 21																				

Figure 5: To start a program of meditation, it is best to meditate everyday—even if for only a few minutes. Above is a table showing how you can start by meditating for just 5 minutes a day, and by increasing your time by just one minute a day, in three weeks time you will be up to 20 minutes.

Place a check mark on this chart where you wish to start, beginning with day 1. Increase your time gradually by just 1-2 minutes a day, until you are up to 20 minutes.

Spiritualized Sex

In the last quarter of this past century, we have seen a sexual revolution that has changed the face of our nation. We have seen free love in the 1960s, a plea for equal rights in the 1970s, acceptance of homosexuality in the 1980s, and a cry for abstinence in the 1990s. With the hippies came the slogan "make love not war." The seventies encouraged us to explore our sexuality and ask ourselves who we are. The onset of AIDS in the eighties brought about concern for this newfound sexual freedom. The 1990s brought a more conscientious approach to sex, with still an emphasis on self-expression. As we enter a new millennium with gay weddings, fertility clinics, genetic engineering, and surrogate motherhood, we face many moral questions that have our nation sharply divided.

In the midst of this, the New Age generation has reached back into the past and revived a four-thousand-year-old religious practice known as Tantra Yoga and the Kama Sutra. Both originated in Asia as a way of spiritualizing romance. Sex was viewed as something natural and beautiful, like singing or dancing. In ancient India, sex was considered an art form and was one of sixty-four arts that every cultured person learned. Traditional Tantra students spent many years with a spiritual teacher, to understand and master their minds and bodies. It was understood that a person's sexuality was an intricate part of who they were.

Today many tantric groups, classes, and books have appeared. Skeptics say that these groups are really little more than a revival of the love-ins of the 1960s. Proponents of these teachings, however, claim they allow us to harness our passion and elevate our spirit. Our passions are harnessed first by learning to meditate and experience our sexuality as a deep regenerative force. Then, with a partner, by deliberately prolonging foreplay and not releasing sexual energy through orgasm, this passion can be redirected toward a higher spiritual experience.

Tantra says that by recognizing our partner as a manifestation of God, we further focus our energy toward a higher spiritual ideal. Since sex often results from an underlining tension, Tantric lovers were taught to relax with each other during sex. When there was no tension, an orgasm could be delayed for hours, or even days. In Tantra, too much excitement is considered a waste of energy. Instead you relax and let go to the energy that is inside of you. In Tantra, lovemaking is actually a prayer, where you are directly experiencing God's love. Here lovemaking is transformed into a sacrament.

Critics of this philosophy encourage a restrictive attitude toward sex, perhaps out of a concern that sex might prompt us to behave in a harmful way. Tantra says that is why we must learn meditation and self-control first. Sex being such a powerful drive has prompted many people to sacrifice their families and self-respect. While many are skeptical of these practices, others contend this seems very reasonable when you consider it is God who created our body, life, sex, and partner. Tantra is really about recognizing that God is even our desire, including sexual desire, and it is about transforming sex into a spiritual experience.

Transmutation

Tantra teaches that instead of making a natural desire like sex a sin, we must eventually rise above all of our desires. These ancient teachings caution us, moreover, to avoid things that tempt us to behave carelessly or selfishly. Tantra says our drives are not wrong in themselves, and this energy can eventually be transformed into a desire for something else—something spiritual if we choose. It calls upon the use of our bodies and senses to produce spiritual effects. This philosophy further says it is not the act in and of itself that is wrong but the intention behind the action. For example, even killing someone can be done for very different reasons—out of anger or hatred, in self-defense, or accidentally. It is our intention and motivation that are important insofar as any spiritual consideration is concerned. In this yuga we must also be careful to protect ourselves against unprepared pregnancies and disease.

Yoga

Tantra is one of several forms of yoga. Yoga begins by teaching us we must first avoid certain things if we can't control our urges. A simple example is someone who wants to quit a habit such as smoking. He or she may need to avoid places where people smoke. This person may also need to deliberately stop him- or herself at every thought of having a cigarette. After a while, ex-smokers may be able to go wherever they want without being tempted to smoke. In the same way, yoga says that until we achieve control over an impulse, we must continue to use caution. Gradually, through this conscious approach we develop self-control.

This is similar to raising a child. At first you may need to discipline a child until he or she learns self-control. For example, it is dangerous for a child to play with matches. We recognize we need to keep matches away from a child. However, a mature person can use the same match to cook food or make a fire to heat the house. A mature person knows how to control the flame.

In yoga one practices control over one's thoughts and desires, until you are in a position to sense what's appropriate in any given situation. Once we have achieved self-control, Tantra says we are able to enter into sex without fear of what we may feel or do. It emphasizes, however, these teachings are not for those who haven't developed self-control.

When we can observe our sexual impulses and desires, feeling free to act or not act, then we have transcended the act itself, and it can become meditative. In the example of smoking, when smokers can become completely aware of what they are doing—of the actual effects of their smoking—their bodies will normally reject the smoke. In other words, if you can become completely aware of your body while you are smoking you will realize that your lungs, throat, and heart don't want the cigarette. The more conscious we are, the easier it is to transcend something if we need to.

Devotional Energy

The next most important thing in Tantra is a strong spiritual inclination. It is important that a student of this discipline have a sincere love and devotion to God. Tantra says that our sexual desire can fuel anything, including spiritual devotion, and it can lift us toward a higher spiritual state. As we will discuss later, this devotion is vital for the practice of Tantra, just as steering a car is essential to driving it.

Prana is the Hindu word for energy, of which all living things are made. The Hindus believe everything is created from prana. Our body's own energy travels primarily along a central nervous system (CNS). In yoga, there is a spiritual energy known as the Kundalini, which underlies the physical energy. It runs through a spiritual channel along the spine, which is called the *sushumna*. The Kundalini energy is described as being like a snake coiled around the spine and climbing its way up to higher spiritual centers, or *chakras* (see page 55). Different expressions of this energy correspond to various energy centers in our body. All of our energy comes from this central energy source, and since sex is a strong biological drive, this energy can be extremely useful.

A strong sexual drive can, for example, be transformed into an enthusiasm for God. These teachings suggest we can learn to use sexual energy to maximize our spiritual devotion. For example, certain devotional activities can raise our energy. You can increase your spiritual energy a great deal through prayer, singing, and dancing, and use it to expand your consciousness. This redirecting of energy happens all the time. Athletes will focus all their attention on preparing for a race, leaving little or no attention to devote to anything else, including sex. A musician, painter, or writer may also express their lovemaking energy through this creative self-expression.

Male and female

Our own individual nature is both male and female. The sexes are really two halves of a whole. In reproduction, for example, one becomes two and two become one. An egg and sperm cell merge and produce one being, although it still contains both parts. According to Tantra, it is through realizing and integrating both our parts that we feel fulfilled. This wholeness creates a complete energy. The Rosicrucians believe that the sexual union of male and female can form a powerful current, or "union of magnetism." Whenever these two forces merge, whether on a cosmic or microscopic scale, they complete each other. Separate, they are always incomplete.

This initial split into two halves is also seen in pairs of opposites, such as positive and negative, light and dark. When we experience our whole nature, we see the sexes are complementary, like two sides of the same coin. Tantra says sex can lead us to the experience of this sacred union, a feeling of integration between ourselves, God, and another. It can also help us to develop a relationship based more on mutual love, respect, and spiritual growth.

Tantric Sex

In the throngs of passion you may have experienced moments when all boundaries seem to dissolve between you and your lover. You may feel you have melted together. Usually these experiences are brief. However, through Tantra we can increase the intensity and frequency of these moments. By deliberately holding in our sexual energy, we can gather it and prolong our lovemaking.

A simple way to get a sense of Tantra is to find a secluded place with your lover. (If you do not have a lover, you can do this by yourself—just imagine a partner.) Meditate together and ask God to become a part of your lovemaking. Ask for God's divine presence during your time together. Recognize your partner as a living manifestation of God, of the male or female aspect, or both. Since God has assumed all forms in our universe, you can recognize that God is certainly present in your partner. Start by sitting and facing each other, and holding each other's hands. Gaze gently into each other's eyes. For a few minutes just sit in a room, perhaps with candles and incense.

Get in sync with your partner's breathing. Breathe together. When one of you exhales, the other exhales. Inhale together. Look into each other's eyes. If you notice your body starting to move or sway, just allow it to. This will start to blend your energies together. Your eyes may blink but continue looking into your partner's eyes. After ten minutes or so, close your eyes and allow any swaying to continue for a few more minutes. Breathe as if you and your partner are the same person.

Then take some time to enjoy each other, caressing and kissing each other, without completing sex. Do not undress or move any further into lovemaking unless you can do so without achieving orgasm. Practice this for several days, just going as far as you can each day. Each time you may go a little further into lovemaking, so long as you can resist having an orgasm. In your mind do not move ahead to an outcome; stay in the act, in the moment. Eventually, you can even have intercourse without having an orgasm. Don't think about sex, just let it happen. At first, practice this while you are in a calm and serene mood. Within a short time, you will learn to control your increased energy.

Transformation

You can really begin to feel this accumulated energy—it is very invigorating—and you can feel it inside of you all day. The more intense it becomes, the more it can be used as devotional energy. As this powerful energy moves up the sushumna, it activates the higher centers of awareness and understanding. At first it may be difficult to know if you really need to have an orgasm or not. When any edginess or frustration comes, sometimes you can work through this feeling by praying, singing, and dancing. You can get into a space where you transcend the tension by letting go, then refocusing the energy. The more sexual your nature, the more slowly you may need to proceed, but the more energy you will eventually have at your disposal.

At times it may be best not to build up more energy and perhaps even release it in lovemaking. Before you go to this stage be sure to use protection and proceed only if this is an appropriate relationship for both of you in every important way. With the right partner you can eventually merge in bliss and transcend any sense of separateness. Ask any couple who are really "in love," and they are liable to tell you they experience moments when they feel as if they are "one with each other."

You may experience this as a deep feeling of integration, and afterward you won't feel empty at all. It is a very profound, synchronistic feeling. Wait for that, and if it doesn't happen, there is no need to follow through with an orgasm each time. Instead, enjoy a deeper level of energy that arises inside you. It might take days, or weeks, but begin to hold in this energy, and when certain moments come, this energy will have tremendous capacity to carry you to new heights. Tantra is about transforming our lovemaking from a state of "doing" to an experience of "being." With your partner there must be respect and trust; it is important that both of you work together. If one person chooses to refrain from an orgasm, that doesn't mean the other person can't have one. You just need to accept what the other person needs. Obviously, this won't work if I say, "I won't let you have an orgasm, because I've decided this is what we should do." In Tantra, you don't control the other person but rather you help each other to experience a deeper transcendental joy.

Figure 6: This is the symbol for a medical staff or doctor. Notice that the two intertwined snakes are going up the staff. The snakes represent the "snake like" energy of the Kundilini. It is seen here going up the Sushumna, or spinal column. Notice the angel wings, and the angel head at the end of the staff. This shows that the energy is ascending toward a higher spiritual consciousness. The snakes also represent the positive and negative forces of nature (the Yin and Yang).

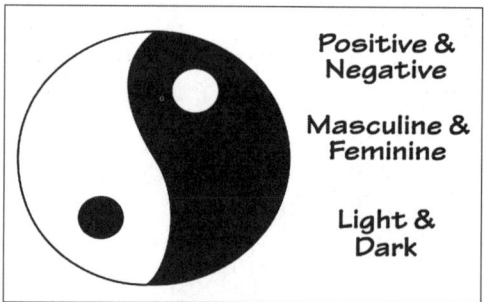

Figure 7: The Tao symbol **above**, represents the aspect of duality in our universe. It is seen symbolically here in its opposites, of light and dark, or positive and negative. In Tao these opposites

are known as the *Yin* and *Yang*. And, it is together that these polarities form a whole. The spot in each, shows also that there is some of each in the each other. They are really a mirror or reverse image of the same reality.

Royal Secret

In Tantra all aspects of life are to be witnessed and accepted for they are all manifestations of God. We are not with God just in heaven but each day of our lives. We are God's children. Everything is God's creation, and we can experience God's presence right here and now. The "royal secret" according to Krishna in the Bhagavad Gita[14] is that God's essence has become all the things in this universe. Everything is God. Our own life arises from God's essence. Krishna reminds us that this doesn't mean our ego, or what we call "me," is God in its entirety. The "me" is an infinitesimal aspect of God, like a single star in a brilliant night sky. Yet each of us is an essential part of the divine whole—and none other than God has become each of us. We *are* God's essence, masquerading as somebody. The trick is to see beyond our "somebody-ness." Within us resides the same consciousness that governs the whole of existence. Every person or molecule is a microcosm of a cosmic whole. These scriptures say, therefore, it is natural we should enjoy harmony with God, others, the universe, and ourselves.

Tantric Philosophy

When people first hear about the philosophy of Tantra, they assume it is saying that we can do anything we want—especially when it comes to sex. Well, you always can do what you want, but Tantra says there are simply going to be certain consequences to everything we do. Instead of condemning or making excuses, we need to accept full responsibility for our lives. In Tantra, you accept everything—whatever it is. For instance, if someone is hurting you, rather than saying this person is evil, you simply take whatever steps are necessary to protect yourself. Whether this means defending yourself, running, or calling the police, there is no need to allow others to hurt you. In this philosophy, you negate nothing, including yourself. It is a path of acceptance through heightened awareness. Jesus said, "Judge not, so ye be not judged."

Another example is if a small child were playing with a gun, what would you do? Wouldn't you educate the child as to the dangers of guns? Would you suggest to the child that they were evil, simply because they didn't know better? To possibly suggest the child or the child's curiosity is bad might undermine the child's confidence and create self-doubt. If this happens on a regular basis, the child may lose self-confidence and the ability to trust. This has happened to many people especially when it comes to sex. Guilt, shame, and embarrassment have caused many to lose confidence in themselves and in their ability to enjoy sex. Tantra says we must totally accept ourselves at each moment and bring to each moment our full awareness.

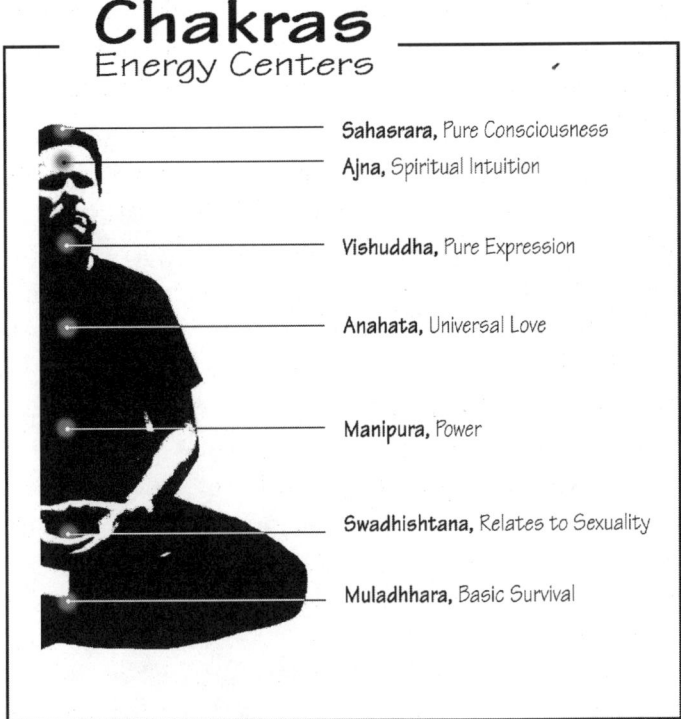

Figure 8: Energy circulates throughout our entire body at all times. However, when it is particularly concentrated in a certain spot, or *Chakra*, then the activity associated with that chakra is enhanced. For example; A strong need for survival is located at the base of the spine, and this is called the *Muladhhara chakra*, and this includes the flight or fight response. During sexual stimulation the *Swadhistana chakra* is activated. When we say we have a "gut feeling" about something, this corresponds to the energy center located in the solar plexus called the *Manipuri chakra*. When we say we "felt it in our heart," this relates to the *Anahata chakra* that corresponds to the area near the heart. When we say "the words just flowed out of my mouth," this is energy expressed through the *Vishuddha chakra*, in the throat. When we experience a greater sense of intuition and knowledge, the *Ajna chakra* (all-seeing eye) is stimulated in the forehead. And when we feel a sense of oneness and synchronicity, this is the experience of energy at the top of the head, or *Sahasrara chakra*.

Life After Death

One of the most interesting research studies I've come across on the subject of life after death is by Raymond Moody, M.D. In his book *Life After Life*,[15] Dr. Moody discusses the many consistencies, or "core experiences," of life after death, as reported by more than 150 patients. All signs of life had left these patients and they had been pronounced dead, yet each had eventually came back to tell their story of the beyond. Dr. Moody calls these *near death experiences*, or NDEs. Some of these patients died in accidents, and others from chronic medical illnesses. They often described a feeling of being outside their body at the moment of death, and floating above their body. They realized *they* haven't ended, but they are no longer their body. There is no limitation of time and space—but rather they were limited by their knowledge or imagination.

Suppose a beam or tree came down and struck you on the head. If you were to die, according to these NDE patients, you are apt to find yourself floating above your body. You might see someone come along and find your body, or you might see a rescue worker trying to revive you. Next, perhaps you think "what is my mother going to think when she hears of this?" Instantly, you are standing beside your mother, who may be thousands of miles away. The spirit world does not have the same relationship of time and space our world does. Perhaps you try to tell your mother you are there with her, but she cannot hear you. She may, through her intuition, just wonder where you are.

Some of these patients pass into a light after leaving their bodies and see themselves in a paradise or heaven, and in the presence of God. Many of these people experience an overview of their life, seeing everything that has ever happened to them. They describe it as a sort of judgment day, in which they are watching this panoramic view of all the highlights of their life, and feel again just as they felt then. They now see things from a higher spiritual perspective, and they realize God totally loves and accepts them, but can they love and accept themselves for some of the things they have done? They see that despite whatever joy or sadness they have experienced, the most important thing in life is to love others, to put ourselves in another person's shoes, and to forgive others. They realize that until we learn this kind of unconditional love, we eventually leave heaven and come back to earth. They tell us we're here on earth to become a more loving and conscious person. For it is here on earth, with our physical limitations, that we develop a greater self-understanding. They say it is through cultivating the kind of love God has for each of us that we eventually find lasting peace in heaven.

Ghosts

Everything in our physical universe is made up of atoms, or energy. This fact was known as long as 2,500 years ago in India. The Hindus taught that all matter was made up of atoms (or in Sanskrit, *anu*) which are constantly vibrating. They used the movement of these atoms to establish their smallest unit of time, which they called a *kala*. They knew it was actually the same energy (or life force) that becomes a tree, a human being, or anything. Although the soul may appear different in each, the material foundation is still the same energy. The Hindus taught that although all of us appear separate and solid, we are really just God's consciousness vibrating at certain frequencies.

All things start as a thought from God, and when the frequency of a thought slows to an atomic rate, it becomes a physical thing or substance. Any substance can then be presumed solid by something less dense than itself. For example, fog is less dense than your body, but your body is less dense than a rock. And a ghost is less dense than fog. As long as consciousness exists at a certain material frequency, it will continue to manifest "physically." As long as a certain frequency is conceived of, it will continue to exist. It exists simultaneously as a whole, and yet also appears to dissipate, and integrate, blending completely, and leaving no trace of separateness at the same time. The Hindus knew there were these different planes to existence, which are relative.

Of the fifty trillion cells in our bodies, Dr. Chopra says in his book *Quantum Healing:* "Ninety-eight percent of the atoms in your body were not there a year ago. The skeleton that seems so solid was not there three months ago. . . . The skin is new every month. You have a new stomach lining every four days . . . a new liver every six weeks."[16]

Dr. Chopra reminds us all matter is 99.9999 percent empty space. Perhaps a simplistic way to think of this is what we think exists *physically* is really only about 0.0001 percent existent. The rest is empty space. When it gets just a little less dense and becomes 100 percent empty space, it has reached the zero-density level, which we call the spirit world, or simply consciousness.

Dr. Chopra tells us atoms are not material objects, but they are vast empty spaces, with fluctuations of energy occurring. He tells us if we could see a particle at the atomic level, we would see energy simply appears from a vast empty void and then dissipates back into the void. In other words, our physical world is really just a fluctuation, or field of energy, that ranges from the more dense physical manifestation of cells and atoms to an increasingly fainter or less dense state. These layers of energy surrounding a thing, from dense to extremely subtle, exist simultaneously. Sometimes when a very faint energy field is seen surrounding a person, it can appear as a halo or a light. Once our body dies, this subtle energy field may continue to resemble us for someone. A ghost can actually be consciousness manifesting itself through this very delicate, remaining energy.

Past Lives

The theory of past lives also suggests we consist of a body and a spirit—and that our body lives only temporarily, but our spirit is everlasting. Spirit is the real everlasting you. For example, if you write a sheet of music, a poem, or a story—it is the paper, ink, and the shape of the letters that are the physical part of your creation. If you burn the poem, have you burnt the poet? No, the spirit of the words and the person behind them are not harmed because the *real you* is not the paper. In this analogy, our body is like the physical paper, but our spirit is what writes it—and it is the one that is behind it. Once a poem is completed, you may write another.

Similarly, once your body is gone, your spirit can represent itself through another body. Another example is to imagine you are casting a shadow on the ground. Your shadow may move with you and it is an image of you, yet you are not your shadow. In this example, your shadow is like your body, but the real you—your spirit—is what casts the shadow. This pairing of your soul and body is what happened at the time of our present birth.

Our soul remembers all of its lives, just as you can remember what happened yesterday. However, each new life is just one more chapter in the life of our eternal soul. Patients who have experienced death tell us they lose the consciousness that was operating through their body (which is where we are normally conscious from while we are awake), and they experience the spirit world. In the spirit world only spiritual laws apply.

The physical laws of substance, time and space have no reality. From this perspective, unity, love, and knowledge are seen as the most essential things. From the light of our spirit, our soul is aware of its relationship with God, and it realizes whether it has lived its life on earth in a spirit of love. Looking back on our lives from this vantage point, we can see that it is when we have truly loved others, God, and ourselves, with all our heart, that we have experienced true joy. Our soul understands the significance of each of our lives and the lessons we are learning from each. When a person has a past life or near death experience, he or she may suddenly experience the spirit world. When they wake up, or they are resuscitated, they come back through the consciousness of their body. In the ancient Indian Bhagavad Gita it says:

> "As the Soul, wearing this physical body, experiences the stages of infancy, youth, adulthood, and old age, even so will it, in due time, pass on to another body, and in other incarnations it will live again, and move and play its part. Those who have attained the wisdom of the nature of the Spirit, know these things, and fail to be distressed by that which comes to pass on earth, in this world of change; to such people 'Life' and 'Death' are but words, and both are but superficial aspects of our deeper Being. Our senses, through their appropriate faculties of our mind, give us reports of cold and heat, pleasure and pain. But these changes come and go; they are shifting, transient and inconstant. Bear them with equanimity, bravely and patiently.... These bodies, which act as enveloping coverings for our souls occupying them, are only physical things of the moment, and not the real person at all. They vanish as all physical things do. Let them go.... Take this into your inner mind, the real person, the spirit of the person, is neither born, or does it die. Unborn, undying, ancient, perpetual and eternal, it hath endured and will

endure forever. The body may die, be destroyed completely, but the soul that has occupied it remains unharmed.... As a person throws away their old clothes, replacing them with new and brighter ones, even so the spirit dwelling in the body, having given up its physical body, enters into new bodies that are newly prepared for it."[17]

In past life hypnosis, clients have told me they see themselves between lives and even in other worlds. Some people see themselves as a bright luminous being. They feel completely at peace, as if they have found their true self. They may see themselves among other glowing souls or departed friends—sometimes floating on a cloud or in a beautiful radiant garden. Others see themselves on distant planets, speaking with God, or learning telepathically with others.

Investigations into past lives

The mystery of past lives became even more intriguing when several of my clients told me of their own investigations into a lifetime they had remembered. One woman said she had gone to a church that provided a computer, allowing her to trace a name back along a family tree. She entered the name, date, and town of the person she had remembered herself to be in a past lifetime. To her amazement, the past life family she had seen herself belonging to was listed in the church's historical records, right down to the same names for all of the family members, their age differences, dates, and towns where they had lived. Apparently, we usually don't remember these previous lives because our present conscious awareness begins at birth, when we first begin to store impressions in our brain. We may think our brain's memory is all we have ever known; however, it is in our unconscious mind where these past life recollections are remembered (this mind exists both before, during, and after our body, and it is everlasting). Hypnosis can allow us to bypass the conscious mind to recall our soul's unconscious memories.

My clients also believed that these past lifetimes often explained why they have a certain talent or ability. For example, someone in this life who has been a good pianist from an early age, might find under hypnosis that they remember a former lifetime learning to play the piano. Or, a person who has had a very difficult time in a marriage in a previous life might in their present life come back with a strong apprehension toward marriage. Just as we gain new experiences in each day of our lives, in this same way, we come back to earth life after life to continue this learning process.

Life on Other Planets

I have had clients who also claim they have lived on other planets during one of their lifetimes. The descriptions of some of these worlds are very similar to that of earth. Interestingly enough, in these worlds when they are aware of what's important, they see what we call spiritually important is the same on other planets. They see God has created all the planets and the earth is just one destination for the soul.

At first these planetary stories seemed provocative to me, and then I remembered in the East they also believe there are many other planets where a soul can be born. There are descriptions of these planets in the Srimad Bhagavatam scriptures. When they speak of life on other planets, they are not just referring to alien life forms, but planets similar to the earth, with life forms and souls the same as ours. They tell us this is why there is no need for us to worry where souls will go if life becomes extinct on earth. In fact, they tell us there are souls like us living on other planets right now. The real issue is not whether life on earth will end—because science tells us life on all planets eventually ends—it is a question of whether we respect this planet God has given to us. When we do not take care of our earth, it reflects a spiritual problem in our consciousness. When our earth eventually does end, the Hindu scriptures reassure us, there will remain many other destinations for us to visit.

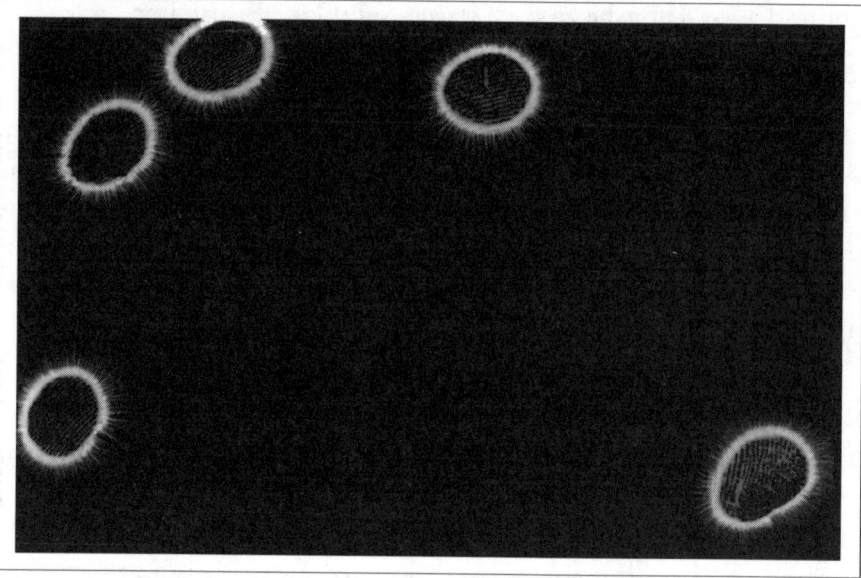

Figure 9: This photo is of fingertips resting on a special plate, which captures a picture of their energy field.

Our physical body is made up of energy, which is actually an electrical impulse. This energy also gives off a light, or aura, around our body. Scientists believe these auras can be photographed with what is called a Kirlian camera. This camera is capable of showing the light given off by our bodies, which is usually not visible to our eyes—just as some sounds may be outside our normal range of hearing, yet still heard on occasion. Likewise, this light can be observed occasionally, even with the naked eye. When an electric current is applied to a special photographic plate (see Figure 9), the aura of some fingerprints is soon revealed. Changes in the character and color of an aura can reflect changes in our consciousness, mood, energy level, or health.

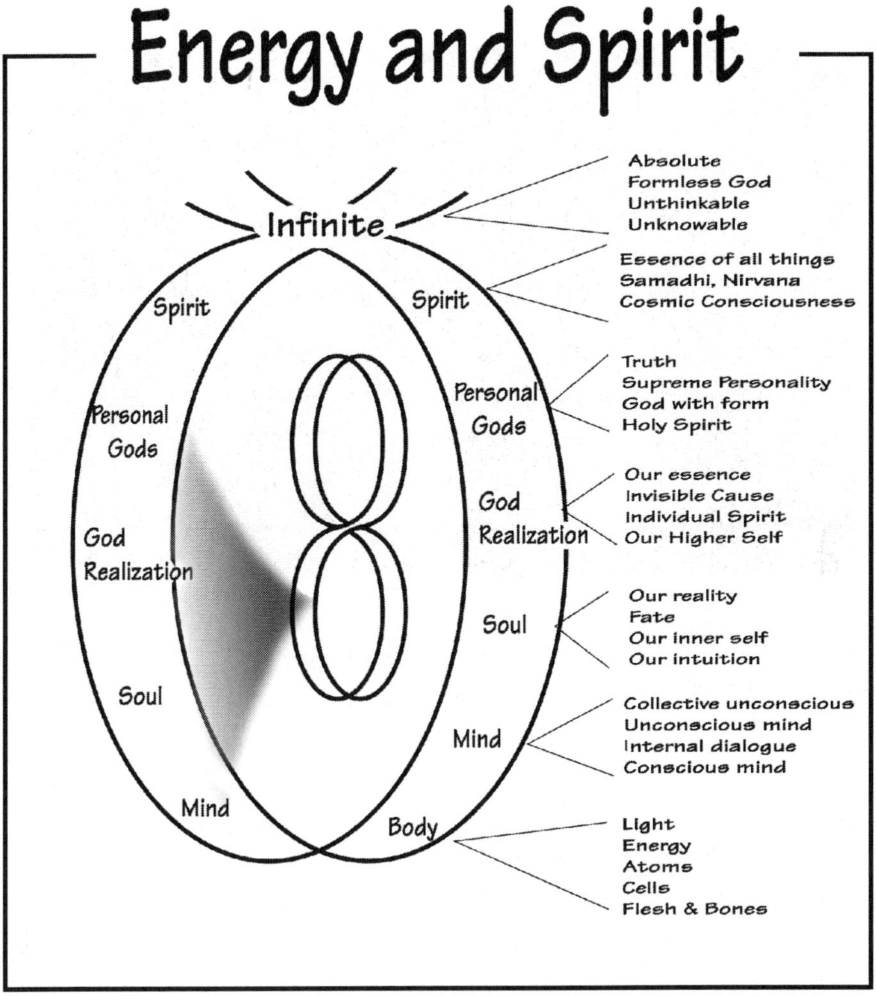

Figure 10: The above chart is an example showing a perspective of God and consciousness—from the highest integrated awareness, all the way down to consciousness as it manifests as our flesh and bones—and then it goes back to the infinite again.

ZERO POINT

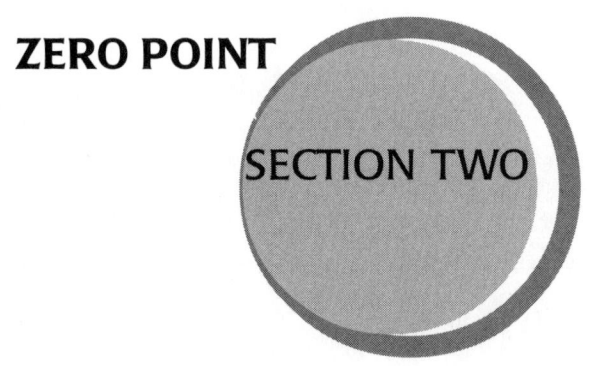

Questions

Do You Know Where Your Mind Is?

The following chapters are based on talks that took place after group-guided meditations.

The state of mind of participants in these meditations is somewhat dream-like. Most are very relaxed but alert at the same time. While we are awake, scientists tell us our mind normally operates at a certain conscious frequency or rate. This can be measured on a machine called an electroencephalograph. When our mind and thoughts slow down, and yet we are aware of what is transpiring in our thoughts, an increased awareness of ourselves or our life may be experienced. Dreaming, meditation, and our subconscious mind all occur at these lower cycles of our brain waves. As our brain waves slow down, if we don't remain aware and alert, we fall asleep.

One participant noticed why he had been in a certain mood lately, noticing himself in a larger sense of the word—more like self-awareness. He became very relaxed, less intent on maintaining a certain outlook. When questioned why he maintained this outlook in the first place, his response was, "I feel I have to believe in something, maybe to feel secure."

"What establishes what you believe in?"

"What I've been taught and told," the participant responded. "Probably my background mostly. How far can we actually slow our minds down? And what happens then?"

If we are aware at the moment the activity of the mind completely ceases, our thoughts stop, then we are no longer our mind at that instant. We are no longer what we usually call "us" with all our associations. A more expansive consciousness is experienced, beyond us, said to be ultimately universal and collective. Our own consciousness is a part of this collective consciousness.

Science tells us our own subjective outlook is formed by our senses as they collect data based on their function and limits of receptivity. Stimuli such as sound, sight, touch, smell, and taste, are interpreted by our mind based on past associations, concepts, language, interpretations, values, and impressions—both conscious and unconscious. In response to our perception of the events of our life we create our own view of life's laws and principals. For example, my senses tell me that the earth is stationary, and the sun moves across our sky. However, we know this is an illusion.

Our mind is like a snowball rolling downhill. It collects impressions through time. When our mind makes a decision it is usually based on our past associations. The scriptures tell us there is a faculty of our consciousness beyond our mind, which when utilized, allows us to become less and less bound to our individual experience, and eventually merges with the universal consciousness. It is on the way we meet this dispassionate witness within us that can observe ourselves or something outside ourselves in an objective light. It is not so predisposed to the me, or the ego.

How do we *know* this is true? Regardless, one must find out if it is true for oneself. Certain people repeatedly observe information and insight about themselves and others, without even being present or having any other way of knowing. Police departments have relied on using people with this inner sight to locate missing persons. People have been tracked down in obscure places, thousands of miles from where a person has perceived their whereabouts. This dimension of our consciousness beyond our own mind, when experienced, provides us with unbiased information independent of our own personal experiences.

Although teachers and educators can teach us about this awareness, most of the time we are told about something from the past based on someone else's impressions. It is a moment frozen in time formulated from *their* personal subjective experience, rather than our own spontaneous awareness. Even if someone's observation is objective and accurate at the moment, it is relevant to a specific momentary experience, and we will have to look for the truth of the next moment in that moment itself. Even things that seem constant, like the sun, are slowly changing. Scientists tell us that stars go through a stellar evolution, eventually becoming what are referred to as "red giants" and then "white dwarfs." The fact of the sun, however, can be observed in each relative moment.

This brings us to the question, how could one know anything if one knew everything? Imagine if you had the time and funds to travel anywhere in the world. You would still be somewhere, one place or another, at any given moment, whatever your itinerary. Just as the clouds float in the sky, our mind floats in a background of pure impartial consciousness. We have probably all had the experience of true clarity at sometime, as if the clouds have passed or a light bulb has gone on. Something has come to light, and our thoughts seem very lucid, as though the dialogue in our head has stopped. We feel very calm and relaxed at these moments.

The meaning of life, then, is to *be* life. Anything is what it is—a blade of grass, a bird, a human being. Meaning implies someone's personal perspective. The actual meaning of a bird is being a bird. If one asks what the meaning of a rock is, one might say, "Well, obviously to simply be a rock. It's the result of a long geological process. It has certain characteristics, and it interacts with everything else in a way relative to its nature." If one asks the same question about a bird, one may answer in a similar way.

But when it comes to people, we tend to think we are in a separate category. If we learn simply to observe the dynamics of our own thinking, as though we were witnessing someone else, then we can see clearly and objectively our own human characteristics and tendencies. Certainly, we have as much right as anything else to be here. And, it is the way of nature for life to emanate from other life. However, a recognition of the balance and value of all life forms is now becoming very important in our world.

Any life can be seen from many perspectives. From a behavioral point of view, a biological standpoint, a cellular perspective, and so on. Systems, within systems, within systems. Realities within realities. Examined partially, there arises a perspective and, therefore, a meaning. All life is ultimately collective. A synchronized whole, a unity of energy, consciousness, and spirit. What is my meaning? To be my unique me. Relative to my meaning, I create my God, my universe, my world, all from my perspective. What is beyond meaning? Unity, freedom, and wholeness.

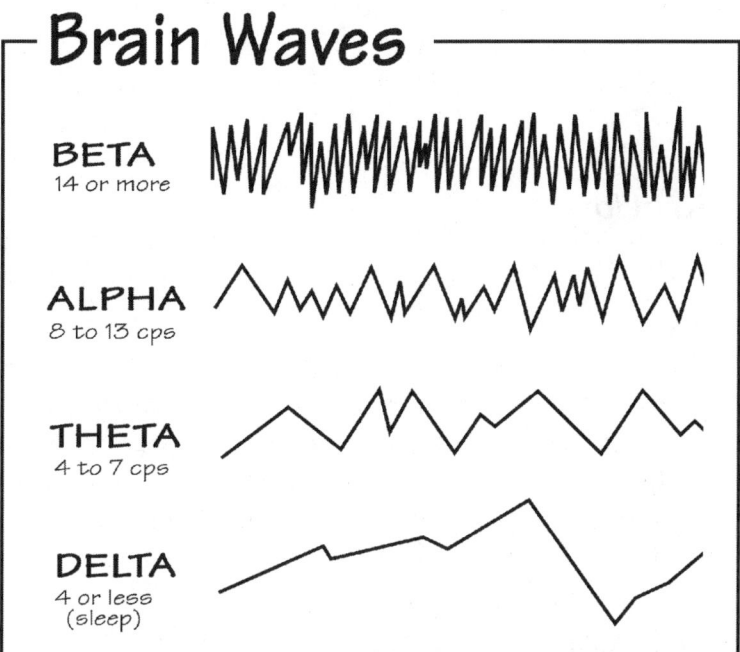

Figure 11: While awake, our brain's electrical activity operates at a certain rate, which is represented at the top of these electroencephalograph (EEG) readings. Our waking state rate is known as *beta*. These brain waves are recorded by electrodes placed at specific locations on the scalp. These levels, or waves, represent the changing bioelectric voltage, as the brain waves slow down from beta to *delta*.

Progressive relaxation produces smaller undulations and slower brain waves. As the mind reaches increasingly deeper levels, the EEG waves become larger and the quality of consciousness becomes lighter.

These slower rhythms can be experienced while we are aware and alert, often during meditation and hypnosis. *Beta* represents our normal conscious state. *Alpha* characterizes a relaxed drowsy state (hypnosis and meditation begin here). *Theta* denotes dreaming, deep meditation, and hypnosis. *Delta* is deep sleep, when we are totally at rest.

Religion
by Misty Flatt

*The water flows
from a river deep
to be rejoined in the ocean
to be complete
many rivers there are
none of them the only one
all unique in their form
for this is how it is done
different rivers to make different pathways
and back to their source
for all have a divine purpose
on their flowing course
once the waters merge
they realize their essence is the same
their journey was accomplished
merely by different names.*[18]

Where Is God Today?

What Is God?

The scriptures tell us before the existence of life and the galaxies, there was God. God is everything that exists. God is omnipresent, present in all places at all times. God is omnipotent, almighty, and has complete authority and influence. In the beginning, it is said, there was God alone. God contained nothingness, yet all that could ever be was within this void. God was beyond both this nothingness and all that could ever exist. God conceived thought and energy into this emptiness. These thoughts were the laws of creation. God's energy, directed by these principals, set this infinite reality through nature into time and space.

The scriptures also tell us God is the Supreme intelligence of the universe. The divine consciousness has conceived of energy and its dynamics, and created all things from itself. We are all manifestations of God, a part of a cosmic whole. Imagine, for example, you are slicing a lemon. You can slice it into many parts, but each part is a member of the whole. Each part is none other than the lemon itself and has a specific relationship to each of the other parts. Each part is essential to recreate the whole. If any piece were missing, the lemon would be incomplete. The true nature of each part is that it combines with all its other parts to form a whole. We cannot say that each piece is exactly the same since each cut may vary in size, shape, and angle. Each does, however, constitute the same ingredients and has a common source. It isn't necessary to taste each piece of a lemon to know its tartness, scent, and color.

God is the Holy Spirit, the essence, the original cause of all things. Our souls emanate from this spirit. Each person's soul is, in essence, the same although they appear different given every individual's own personal perspective. For instance, you might behave one way when you are at work, but you act differently when you are with your lover, family and friends, or casual acquaintances. You may also dress differently, depending on the situation. But it is still you.

In the same way, the spirit has assumed the form of all the different souls, each being none other than the Holy Spirit itself. In our lemon analogy, God is the lemon, or universe. The one cutting the Lemon, and what's more, God has a whole orchard of lemon trees stretching as far as the eye can see. Each tree heavy with lemons.

For those who have trouble identifying with the spirit as our essence, consider these examples: When you wake up from a dream, no matter how real it seemed, how long does your disorientation last once you are awake? In the same way, the spirit is not unfamiliar with itself.

Imagine you are an actor. You study your part, rehearse your lines, and really put your heart into the role. On the final day of shooting, after the last scene, you walk off the set. You no longer have to be that person or play that part. No matter how sincerely you portrayed that character, you go back to another reality that is just as familiar and perhaps more real than the part you had been playing. Both these realities are real to you.

What is the most important thing for us to understand about this? There is no one thing, but I wish everyone would develop an intense yearning to communicate with God and would do so often. Love God. Pray and worship God with all your heart! We spend so much of our attention on our work, families, friends, hobbies, etc., but how often do we recognize God and give thanks? It is God who has created all these things and who sustains our very existence.

God will reveal everything to us if we simply ask. "Knock and the door shall be opened," Luke 11:9. We don't have to be formal or worry about what to say. God knows each of us thoroughly. This is why sometimes when we think we need something, it *isn't* what we need most, and God knows.

We can all realize our inner nature and sense our relationship with God first by seeing ourselves as we are, then through prayer and meditation. The knowledge that deep inside we are interrelated with every other thing is already within each of us: "God is in each man." We are like the lemon. Its secret is contained within each of its individual cells, its DNA. The whole lemon can be reconstructed from just one of its cells.

"Love thy Neighbor as Thyself."

If you don't love yourself, how can you love your neighbor as thyself? What if one piece of the lemon says, "I wish I were a thinner wedge"? A thinner wedge of what? The same stuff, just thinner? Or perhaps one wedge looks at a bigger wedge and says, "Now I wish I was like that!" What is a bigger wedge, except the same stuff but larger? Sometimes, you cut a piece in a certain shape to place on the rim of your water glass or to place on the edge of your plate. Likewise, God creates us in different forms.

Are You Trying to Be a Prophet?

I am really a philosopher. I have no special authority. I am just like anyone else, sharing my thoughts, based on my own experience in meditation.

Where Do We Usually Get Lost?

Most of us do think primarily about ourselves. We feel separate from most things. This is consistent with the impression we get from our physical senses and the message we get from others. As a result, we start thinking about the things we want, such as money, possessions, self-importance, attention, and so on. Our mind eventually craves whatever we dwell on. Through repetition of an impression, we begin to accept it as fact, to the exclusion of who we really are—in essence, a free spirit.

This self-preoccupation leads to an increase in self-centered thoughts and an exaggerated sense of self-importance.

A subtle insecurity also exists because we know deep down this sensory pleasure is not our ultimate fulfillment and doesn't last long. We know we will need something more to sustain this feeling of satisfaction. It can become an addiction. We cannot find lasting peace and fulfillment as long as it depends on continual ego gratification. When others fail to respond to us the way we want, we are competitive and discontented. Competition and selfishness result from this preoccupation with our own status and power.

Our deepest nature is that of a spirit. Until we experience and live in light of this fact, we sense a lack of complete fulfillment. Moving beyond the individual to the universal is true freedom. Transcending beyond the parameters of our own personal associations and patterns and seeing unity in diversity is knowledge.

What Is the Soul?

The scriptures tell us that our soul is the immaterial essence, for the animation of our individual life. The soul is what gives the body its independent life. Our soul includes our individual consciousness, emotions, feelings, thoughts, and will. Each of our souls, through individualization, appears to have a separate nature and character. Each soul is however, a spark of the infinite spirit, and in its essence, boundless.

According to this explanation, even a rock has a spirit. God is the rock. God has created all things, living and nonliving, from itself. God and spirit are present in everything, or omnipresent. Living things have evolved the characteristics of awareness, reason, feeling, and will. We and the rock are of the same spirit.

Haven't you felt, at some time, as if you, the earth, sky, plants, water, are all one field of energy? Once, I was holding a rock in my hand. I had the feeling the rock was just like my hand, only the energy was moving more slowly.

What, then, is reality? Everything is reality! Dreams are a reality. Things that don't exist are a reality. Do you see what I mean? Suppose I go to sleep and dream I am skiing. In the morning, I wake up and I go skiing. Both are real—the dream and the act of physically going skiing. Now, imagine I assume a friend of mine is also skiing, when actually he is sitting in the lodge with a sprained ankle. When someone asks me where he is, I say he is skiing on the mountain somewhere. Even our misconceptions are real. They are real misconceptions. Everything that exists is reality.

Everything is real. The consciousness of God, the individual consciousness of each person, the universal spirit, each separate soul, energy, and the more than a hundred different atoms are all real.

Is Time What Makes Things Exist?

It isn't time that makes things exist, it is the perception of time that influences our perception of existence. Beyond time, everything is both existent and nonexistent—existent through relativity, and ultimately nonexistent and beyond category. *Being* ultimately is unimaginable through thought. Thought is inherent in time and absent in timelessness. Being is timeless. God is beyond the existent and nonexistent, and synonymous is the creation itself.

Everything that exists in the universe is positive and negative, and also is not. Being and nonbeing is inherent in all things. This paradox is the foundation and support of the cosmos. There is no reality of either, unless there is both. Our essence, or spirit, is eternal and beyond both. Everything in our world is and is not. All that we experience is a fluctuation between these two. It is a symbiosis of something and nothing where creation exists; it is this shadow. We all are and we are not. The part that is, is not; the part that isn't, is.

Each of us, on an unconscious level, knows this paradox. Consequently, to exist is an unsettling experience until you feel comfortable with nothingness, or egoless. The spirit watches over nothingness. Nothingness is merely a beautiful silence to the spirit, interrupted by existence. People who are unaware of the consciousness of spirit fear the onset of this loss of ego as annihilation and miss the serenity and peace of this silence. This nothingness is also ultimate fullness from which all things emerge and dissolve. Beyond this nothingness and omnipresence, is spirit and God.

Through us, existence becomes conscious. Our lives, at any moment in this process of actualization, never cease to be an expression of God itself. It is through this existence that God experiences itself and we can experience the infinite.

If this sounds somewhat unbelievable, perhaps an example will help illustrate this existence and nonexistence. In our physical universe, there are what scientists call "black holes." In space, there are gigantic bodies of gas and dust pulled together by their own gravity into objects such as stars, planets, and moons. Our own sun is a gaseous object gathered by these gravitation forces and powered at its center by its own energy. This energy produces within an outwardly directed force throughout the sun. These two forces, the outward and the inward pull of gravity, resist each other and hold each other in a certain balance for the time being.

Every star eventually runs out of fuel or energy, at which point this resistance is overturned. A continued, inward pull, causes the star to shrink drastically. For example, a star a million times the mass of the earth is squeezed down to a star about the same size as the earth. Larger, massive stars have an enormous pull of gravity so strong, they continue to collapse even after there is no trace of the star left. There is no end to this collapse; it just goes on and on. This collapse is faster than the speed of light, so not even light can escape this void. These black holes devour surrounding stars, sucking them up like a cosmic vacuum.

As if this were not fantastic enough, scientists tell us they do not know what happens to these stars when they disappear.

Nobody knows. It's as if they vanish into sheer nothingness. Here is something that once existed—an enormous star—that is simply absorbed into nothingness without a trace. Scientists believe this energy may be the source that powers the galaxy or may also emerge in another form at another place somewhere within the universe.

Through time, all things appear to exist and then to not exist. Beyond time, in timelessness, all things are both existent and nonexistent, simultaneously.

The Goal of Religion

Religion gives us a forum to communicate with God and express our love, gratitude, and needs. It offers us a fellowship of individuals gathered for the same purpose: to direct our thoughts and heart toward God. Religion reminds us there is a supreme being and a universal consciousness to whom we all belong. Through our participation in religion and our love for God, we communicate with symbols. When we sing and pray, we are offering our gratitude and confession to God.

God is everything, but when we see a cross or beads, divinity often comes to mind. When you kneel before an altar, you may feel you are in God's secret chamber. This symbol we have erected out of our faith can actually draw us into an intimate communication with the Almighty. If you are in church, thinking, "This is the part where I kneel," and your heart is not in it, you might as well pick up your coat and go. But if you have a feeling of love in your heart for God, this is the religious experience, whether it happens in church or in the kitchen.

There are, of course, variations in religion throughout the world, just as there are differences in language, dress, food, and customs. If you are in another country and someone calls the Almighty by a different name, why would that surprise you? They probably call a sandwich by a different name too. When someone has his or her hands clasped, offering a heartfelt prayer toward the heavens, is there any question to whom they are speaking? People have different ways of saying things. Some people sing songs one way and some another. Some bow in one way and some another. God hears everyone's prayers, regardless of the dialect.

Different Beliefs as Described by the Prophets

Imagine for a moment you have never seen the ocean before or heard anything about it. Then you meet someone who is a scuba diver. You ask this person what underwater diving is like and he or she tells you, "The equipment is very heavy, and it is difficult to keep your balance without being knocked over by the waves. If you are not careful, your mask may fill with murky water and prevent you from seeing anything." Then suppose some time later you meet another scuba diver and this person tells you, "Diving allows you to experience a wonderful feeling of weightlessness. You can just float effortlessly through the water, like an astronaut in an antigravity chamber. The water is crystal clear!"

If you have never done any scuba diving yourself, you are apt to believe one of these people must be mistaken about the experience, or perhaps they are not talking about the same activity. But if you are an experienced diver, you immediately know both these explanations are true. They are talking about different aspects or experiences of the same thing. In the same way, prophets of different religious traditions may seem to speak of contradictory spiritual realities, when in fact they are the same.

Through Jesus We Enter the Kingdom of Heaven

Many say if you do not follow Jesus' example and believe in what he has said, you have missed the path to freedom. Jesus is right. By surrendering our life to God, respecting and loving others, and living with truth and goodness, we succeed. Apparently, in his life on earth, Jesus never met any leaders of other religions. If Jesus had met such people, perhaps he would have mentioned them. As Jesus surveyed the other teachers and messiahs in his land, it appears he was aware none of them had attained his vision and knowledge. He tells us the greatest among men he knows of is John the Baptist. It is not possible to say when Jesus realized he was the messiah who was predicted to come, because of our incomplete account of his earlier life. As the account of his ministry begins, we see that he is aware of his destiny.

Surrender Versus Sacrifice

Are these words interchangeable?

You can sacrifice your ego. This is what happens when we surrender ourselves to God. We might say, "God, you are the pilot. I am just the vehicle. You drive, I'll go along with you!" Where is God? You feel God in your heart. God is love. You see God in every living thing. When we cannot sacrifice our whole ego, we auction it off in parts.

"I will spend an hour in church on Sunday." "I will fast on Friday." Any personal act that strengthens our love, is wonderful. I baptize myself in the ocean. I wade out into the water, and I say in my heart, "God, thank you! Please allow this precious water of your ocean to wash away my egoism!" We must remember, however, the significance does not lie in the act. It is in the love within our heart. The more we love God, the more love there is in our flight. Who is a better pilot than God? At that point, who are we? We are God's heart, voice, and eyes. Our ego, we see, is just a front. We are spectators and our egos are actors. God directs the action. When we are enthralled and mystified by God's awesome and spectacular creation, this is the saintly state.

Conclusion

I encourage you to be skeptical about what has been discussed here. Don't believe anything I say. Question everything you believe and everything you hear. Chances are, what you believe now is something someone else told you. Did you question it in the same way you are questioning what I am saying? Or did you hear it when you were younger and simply accept it? If you believe what I say is untrue, then dismiss it and do not give it another thought. However, when we hear something that makes us ask questions, we should not so easily dismiss it. If something feels true, but conflicts with what we believe, it may behove us to examine the new idea more closely.

Figure 12: *Inner space.* These glowing dots are an illustration of what a cluster of atoms looks like, when detected with an electron microscope. All matter is made of these tiny ghostlike particles. An atom has a nucleus in the center and electrons that

orbit in an ellipse around it, like the orbit of the planets around the sun. If you imagine the nucleus the size of a basketball, on this scale, the electron would be the size of a pea some 20 miles away.

A single atom is too small to see, and is almost entirely a huge void, or empty space. The nucleus and electron are really just impulses of energy, and not solid material.

Outer space. Galaxies often occur in clusters, as do atoms. Our sun is just an ordinary star, just one of the 100 billion stars in our galaxy. Our galaxy is just one galaxy among a universe of at least 100 billion other galaxies.

Pictured above is the smallest of all known things, and here the largest. Notice how they appear almost indistinguishable?

Morality in the Twenty-First Century

Morality Today

Morality is determined by our intentions in the present. It is what is in your heart and mind. This involves a range of feelings and thoughts, from love to hate, respect to disrespect, caring to carelessness, and so on. You are simply experiencing your own degree at any time. This can even fluctuate with each moment. If I am acting out of a feeling of respect for you, genuinely concerned with not harming you, and perhaps, not so self-absorbed that I am unaware of how I am affecting you, then I am experiencing my own morality.

The question of moral necessity is relative to the definition of a moral life in our own times. The human mind has developed new complexities. Today, new possibilities exist—such as test tube babies, working unwed mothers, space travel—just to name a few.

Morality changes with our perception. Slavery ended in this country when the perception of the equality of all races was established. Until then, many people were actually convinced slavery was a normal part of life, due to their upbringing and conditioning. The question of the morality of slavery may have never entered their minds. Perhaps the moral question for them was, "How can I be a good slave owner?"

Morality may be *not* doing what others want you to do. You might want me to hit you on the head with a bat, and you might be disappointed if I don't. I must choose. On the other hand, you might want to hit me with the bat. Must I let you? Still, neither of us is more important than the other. We are all important. This is a learning process through which we grow. It eventually requires us to transcend ourselves.

Where morality is concerned, we can simply change our mind, or we can change our perception and awareness. We must first discover ourselves and our own intelligence and faith. In time, through transcending our ego, we can begin to experience a better sense of everyone's mutual realities, and synchronicity. These are the kind of people who don't become more self-absorbed and more concerned with themselves as time goes on.

As a person's awareness grows, they can see life either as a field of competitors they must contend with and struggle against to get what they need and want, or as a challenge to understand themselves better and to blend their needs with those of others. Or for most, some of both.

This difference can depend on whether you are focusing on your separateness or on your essence. Awareness of our essence, or spirit, is an actual awareness of the interrelatedness of you and everything else. You actually see all things are born of this essence and interwoven. Your sense of "me" is necessary either way. It is a question of whether we are predominantly preoccupied with ourselves or aware of the collective role we play in the lives of each other.

The point of this learning process is to see the unity behind the players—yourself as one of them, and be a spectator at the same time. We are all different variations of each other. One person may be a music enthusiast, while you simply enjoy music from time to time. You might feel a little anger and resentment on occasion, while another person is excessively carried away with anger and winds up murdering someone.

You might try to stop a murderer from killing someone. Another person might say, "Let me see if I can understand this person's problem and help him or her rectify it." Someone else, who is less concerned with the life of the murderer and more concerned with the lives of others, might say, "Let's put this person to death so he or she won't hurt anyone else."

So morally, what is right? Whatever is done out of love. You can love someone and still see that death is preferable to their present state. This is the issue to another moral question, that of euthanasia, or putting to death those who are hopelessly ill, for reasons of mercy. These are not questions that have a meaningful answer on a theoretical basis. When actually faced with such life and death issue, we must look carefully at all the considerations, and then deep within our hearts in search of our answer. This is what each of us must do if it is our responsibility to decide.

We don't have a responsibility to decide on every issue, however. For example, on the evening news, there will be reported a case of murder. Within five minutes, there are those watching television who will have already decided the fate of the suspect. Let's say you don't really care about this person, so why bother yourself about his or her death? You may think, "Just execute this person and get it over with." If you do care, your answer may even be the same in the end, but here it is the thoughtfulness and consideration with which you decide that is the distinguishing difference.

Take two people who are standing at the bedside of a dying relative in a coma. They may decide together that it would be best to stop the life support system. One might be sincerely concerned for the quality and dignity of the relative's current life. The other may only be thinking of an inheritance. It is a question of what is in our heart and mind. What are our motivations and intentions? Are we truly acting out of a regard for the well-being of others?

You can't let the bully on the block harm the weak and innocent. Remember, you and a group of your friends can subdue even the biggest bully in your neighborhood! But if each of us scatters and hides in our own yard, the bully will run the neighborhood. You will never know what corner he or she will be lurking behind. So we must gather together for the sake of peace.

Isn't the death sentence the ultimate disregard for human life? No, torture is. Is removing a tumor from your body a disregard for your body or the tumor? What if a doctor says, "A shadow has shown up on one of your X-rays. It may be all right, but perhaps we should remove your organ anyway to avoid worrying about it"? Chances are you would want some further tests to be certain of the diagnosis, before you have the organ eliminated. If you found there was a malignant tumor, which was likely to spread, threatening the life of your entire body, do you have the right to remove it? Even though it is a part of you, does the tumor have a right to survive? Is this a question of your lack of respect for the tumor or necessarily hating it? Do you not have a right to end the tumor?

Thou Shalt Not Kill

In Exodus, it states if a man kills someone, he should be put to death, unless he didn't kill the other person intentionally. It goes on to say if anyone curses his father or mother, they must be put to death! Also, if a man sells his daughter as a servant and she does not please her master, he must let her redeem herself and he has no right to sell her to foreigners.

These examples show that morality must be considered in the context and times in which it takes place. Acts, in and of themselves, are not wrong. It is our intentions based on our mutual expectations that steer our destiny.

All the problems of this world are symptomatic of those that lie within each of us. Our world is a mirror of ourselves. If people resolve the conflict within themselves—their anger, fear, envy, and so on—then conflict would not exist in the world. Rather than think about what everyone else should do—the oil companies, food manufacturers, the courts, the government, my neighbors—if I pay attention to myself, "the man in the mirror," I will be correcting the problem at its source and doing right by example. Why blame others and talk so loud and do so little? Is it because it is easier and less threatening to complain about civic or international problems than deal with the flaws of my own character?

If there is a world or local issue that is important to me—something that reaches within me and prompts me to make a difference—I should follow my heart and act accordingly. This is how the Holy Spirit works through us to influence the world. But why complain about or judge something that I have no real motivation to do anything about?

We all judge. We judge the distance between our car and the one ahead of us, what to do if a friend needs help, how to vote on an issue, and so on. But why find fault just for the sake of blaming others for the problems of this world? Jesus said, "Do not worry about the speck in your brother's eye, until you have removed the beam in your own eye. Then you will see well enough how to remove the speck from your neighbor's eye." There are those who think that they will work on themselves one day—once they have their dream house, a new car, designer clothes, a vacation home in the mountains, and so on. However, with this kind of intention, that day rarely ever comes.

Abortion

Like all things, abortion is not right or wrong in and of itself. These days, abortion is, in most cases, practically unnecessary with our technology for birth control. If we would prevent unwanted pregnancies in the first place, we would have no need for most abortions. Unfortunately, because of fear, lack of understanding, manipulation, and embarrassment, people wind up regretting the consequences of their actions. Frankness, openness, and honesty in education is very important. Parents can unburden their children by removing their own fears and doubts from their children's lives.

If a woman inadvertently becomes pregnant or is the victim of rape, she should be able to decide objectively whether to choose adoption, abortion, or to keep the child. I don't believe abortion is like "playing God"—not any more than extending lives is. In our society, we have used medicine and surgery to prolong lives that would have been lost naturally. Once we take extraordinary measures to prolong life, we have already meddled in the business of life and death. Because of man's technological success in medicine, overpopulation is a critical issue. How many people would hesitate to allow an operation to save their child's life? We have given ourselves permission to save lives, increased fertility, and therefore necessitated the need to control our population, especially of those lives that wouldn't be cared for properly.

Underlying this controversial issue is also a fear of death. Subconsciously, we think, "If someone has the right to decide whether someone else should live, then what's to stop this person from eventually deciding to kill me?" This fear of death is also a part of the euthanasia issue.

Embryos that are aborted cause us confusion, but the Holy Spirit foresees the destiny of each soul and is not surprised by our actions. A soul is not assigned to a body whose destiny it is not to be born. Once an infant is born, the soul has assumed occupancy. And sometimes not even then, in the case of a still birth.

Is Eating Animals for Food Wrong?

Everything is God. An ear of corn, a chicken, a lamb, a tree, a human being, and so on. We are all equally significant. Suppose a tiger attacks and eats you. Is the tiger wrong? Of course not. You cannot live on this planet without destroying other life forms. Even when you take a breath, you are inhaling small organisms. When we walk across a field, how many tiny animals or insects are we crushing under our feet?

It is a question of whether or not we love and respect life. Do we have a feeling of gratitude in our hearts for the life that is sacrificed for our existence? I once said to a friend, "I wish all the animals could roam and graze as nature intended. And if people must kill them for food, that it is done kindly, swiftly, and painlessly."

My friend said, "Do you have any idea how expensive meat would be?"

I said, "Very well, let us pay that price if we want to eat meat and let's spare the suffering of the animals!"

Some spiritual people avoid eating meat and some don't. Some groups don't eat meat, while others eat only certain kinds of meat or fast during certain religious holidays. Native Americans, for example, showed enormous respect and love for animals. They would pray before a hunt and ask God to bless them with the life of an animal. They would also give thanks to God after the hunt. They used every last bit of the animal, including the bones, meat, sinew, and skin. For the Indians, nature was the place where the spirit world expressed itself through the physical world, and people, animals, and spirits were all interwoven together. They would often symbolize their connection with the spirit world by identifying themselves with the characteristics of a certain animal. For example, a bear hide might be thought to lend a warrior the spiritual and physical attributes of the bear, and so on.

It is this kind of purity that makes zoos and over-cutting the forest so appalling. Have you ever been to the zoo and seen the animals pacing back and forth in their cages?

Many people are becoming vegetarians because they are aware of the horrors of the animal industry. There are farms, however, that have "free range" livestock, and they treat the animals with respect. There are also more companies now that do not test their products on animals.

These days, in most parts of the world, it is possible to obtain foods that contain adequate protein without having to eat meat. It is important, however, to include a wide selection of grains, nuts, seeds, peas, rice, beans, legumes, and dark green leafy vegetables in your diet.

In the Bible[19] in Romans it says, "One man's faith allows him to eat everything, but another man, whose faith is weak, eats only vegetables. The man who eats everything must not look down on him who does not, and the man who does not eat everything must not condemn the man who does, for God has accepted him."

Love New Age Style

A Description of Love

Real love is an experience of the unitive state. When you love someone or something, you actually sense you are a part of it and it is a part of you. You are infused with it and can partially or completely lose the experience of separateness when you love.

Love does not own or possess. It is a recognition of our inseparableness. Love is a state of being. You can have a love of the ocean, trees, stars, sunset, birds, and flowers. Everywhere you look, there is beauty.

Marriage can be a very beautiful experience. When we make a commitment to another person, it should reflect a deep conviction that we acknowledge. This is true of any vow. Let's say I vow to raise your son if you should die. What if you die, and I ignore your son and my vow? Then my vow was not true. My vow may have been a temporary sentiment. Marriage provides safety for some. It may help to see certain financial considerations will be met and the needs of children will be considered, if the couple dissolves the relationship.

If you are not mature enough to behave out of love and respect for your partner, then you should have a contract for their sake, and vice-versa. These days, just because you have an agreement "'til death do us part" doesn't mean you will not part from your spouse. Perhaps it will make parting less hasty. Individuals guided by an unselfish nature in such matters, do so with or without marriage. Others might be wise to marry, all things considered.

What about sex before marriage? Marriage is not the determining factor of whether we have a healthy sexual relationship, and sex is not proof that we have a good marriage. A marriage is only as healthy as the participants. Love, kindness, abuse, domination—these are nonpartisan. They affect both married and unmarried couples. The state of your relationship is simply what it is, with or without a legal arrangement. If two people love each other and want to have a legal agreement or not, it's up to them.

Is it wrong to want to have sex before marriage? If I want to have sex with someone, the question is, do I care about the other person's well-being? Is my interest out of a genuine attraction, affection, and respect? Have I portrayed my feelings honestly? Have I considered the consequences? Taken appropriate precautions? Do I care about the consequences to my partner? Do I sense that this is appropriate for them?

You may think, "Am I really going to care about all of that?" Others may think, "Of course I would—that's all very important!" Some people will be hurt by the sex they engage in, married or not. They may feel used or neglected, contract a disease, or acquire an undesired pregnancy. Why? Perhaps they didn't think, or they thought the previous considerations were not important. Others will find a new depth to the meaning of love, of communion with another through sex. Some may experience a brief awareness of a transcendental reality, a release from themselves orgasmically.

If you have sex before marriage and think you shouldn't, then there will be a conflict within you. If you question this idea, its nature and what accounts for it, then regardless of what you decide, you may feel more content with your decision. Sex is not wrong out of wedlock, in and of itself, any more than eating or dancing would be. In our times, God, through science, has offered us the knowledge of how certain diseases are transmitted, effective diagnosis of diseases, and reliable methods of birth control. However, some people are raised to feel embarrassment and fear with regard to their sexual feelings. This inner conflict closes the door to understanding and wise decision-making. Would you jump from an airplane with a parachute you had haphazardly packed? When the physical and emotional risks of sex are so high, isn't it wise to carefully consider your actions?

If one's sexuality is suppressed through fear, it is liable to take an unhealthy form of expression. Many a hypocrite has spoken against sex only to later secretly seek sex in private.

In an earlier chapter, it was suggested that abstinence from sex can heighten creativity and performance. Is this discussion contradicting what was said earlier?

No. If one abstains from sex to heighten the experience, it is out of choice, not conflict. Sexual impulse originates from a spring that also supplies the expression of our will and nurtures transformational change. This same sexual energy can be directed toward the expression of your inner creativity and change. If it is suppressed through conflict, however, and not released in other ways, then before long frustration is likely to result. If a suitable situation or partner is unavailable, masturbation allows for the release of this unused energy.

When we make sex unnatural, hold it in contempt, or suppress it, it will surface eventually and often quite inappropriately. Marriage does not ensure healthy sex out of kindness and love. The only thing that ensures this is kind and loving people.

As for homosexuality, the question is whether the person is kind and loving. Does this person respect his or her partner? Are their actions sincere and based on a concern for the well-being of the other? Our choice of sexual object is deeply anchored in the core of who we are. If we transcend ourselves, we also transcend sex and on occasion, vice-versa.

Sexual arousal is a natural response, but the object and expectations are learned. In one culture, beautiful may be someone with a lower lip stretched to the size of a silver dollar and a rabbit bone through the nose. The appropriate sexual conduct varies between cultures. Once again, our intentions are the determining factor. Perhaps if we went to another culture we might offend someone unintentionally by not understanding their customs. It is our motivation that is important. Sex can be expressed in many different ways. In this respect, it's just like any other human expression.

There is often a negative association connected with sex because of fear, awkwardness, and embarrassment. Sex is one of the strongest drives, and therefore capable of tempting us to do harm to ourselves or another person, where other drives might not. However, someone else might be persuaded to do something dishonest for financial gain. For example, I can express physical energy and drive by working, studying, running, playing, sexual activity, and so on. It's the intention and effect of my energy in any of these areas that is significant. If I run carelessly and fall, I may injure myself. If I run into someone else, I may injure him or her. If I'm playing in a hazardous place, I may get hurt. In sex, as in all things, it is a question of our awareness and intentions. If I engage in sex to conquer or manipulate someone, my actions are going to eventually bring misery to myself and my partner.

We all begin life in a totally dependent state. Without protection, nurturing, and care, we could not survive. How long would we physically survive if we were taken and left in the woods after our birth? We begin our lives as completely dependent beings. This is why the first few years of life are so important. We develop an impression of whether life is mostly painful or pleasurable, safe or unpredictable. Whether we feel accepted or rejected. Cared for or neglected. Whether we are allowed to express ourselves and explore our curious world, or whether we feel controlled and always restrained. Do we feel attractive and desired, or unwanted and unimportant?

It is not difficult to see how these early impressions create the foundation for our future expectations and for our interpretations of the events of our life. This feeling of belonging we experience as infants is diffused and sublimated by our extended family, friends, peers, and acquaintances later in our youth. This feeling of needing to be inseparable from another, however, is not lost. It is retained within our minds, reminiscent of a time from our earliest beginning.

When we fall in love, a configuration of impressions opens a door to our unconscious. Like a flood, we regain this sense of total belongingness with another. Our contact with other acquaintances may also diminish at this time. We often become attached to this object of our love, because we long to experience this feeling and we associate this new person with the experience. You must be vulnerable to fall in love—totally open, without resistance. Spiritually, we are all one. Our physical birth is also symbolic of this fact: therefore, we enter the world through another.

When people fall in love, they often have a sense of the overwhelming personal importance of the experience. Either compatibility of the two personalities involved will enhance this feeling of love, or rivalry and conflict may cause it to fade quickly. We grow through such a relationship. If it ends, however, it can leave the participants feeling abandoned, hurt, or confused. Wondering, "what happened to this feeling of being in love?"

Self-Growth

Change

Change is inevitable. Sudden changes result from an actual alteration in our thinking and feeling toward an existing pattern. Usually, we try to act in a certain way and curb our behavior, and we often conform and do what is expected of us. But where is our authenticity? Do I pretend at first and hope this becomes the real me? In important matters, this approach often leads to hypocrisy and a difficult struggle within ourselves. If I can see a pattern at its roots, in my unconscious, with sufficient incentives, I can change and succeed.

If we ask God with a sincere heart to allow us to make any needed changes, surely God will see that we do so. How can we change something that has become a habit? By correctly identifying a trait and understanding the reason for it. For example, characteristics such as insecurity, anger, argumentativeness, and dishonesty are traits we have developed based on our past needs. If a person was treated unkindly as a child, he or she might have developed a defensive attitude. Now as an adult, with one's childhood abuse over, this person may not automatically let go of this defensive pattern. Even though the threat is gone, it may have become deeply ingrained into their personality.

Since we do things to feel good and to avoid discomfort, we can rightfully link our harmful behavior with the pain it's bringing us and our desired change with our happiness. Say, for example, you are insecure. As a child you were ridiculed by your parents. If you can first understand and become aware of your feelings, you can gradually re-educate yourself to think and respond in a new way. Writing positive affirmations to yourself and taping them to your mirror can help: "I am a beautiful person. I deserve to be happy!" Little by little, negative notions fade through understanding them—not through denial or repression. Before long, these feelings are like an old acquaintance, who is no longer a significant part of your life. In the future, it may be hard for you to believe they ever had the influence on you they did. Whatever we have learned to do, we can learn to do otherwise.

Bad Habits

The more awareness we develop, the more it can bring about change. For example, if you smoke, try to focus on nothing but smoking. Smoke and really be aware of what's happening. Think about why you smoke. Say you started smoking to feel important and grown-up. Perhaps your health is not a key issue at this point. To motivate a change, you could associate through affirmations, both on a conscious and unconscious level, the act of smoking shows immaturity and a lack of self-importance. Associate being a nonsmoker with just the opposite. Perhaps look in a mirror and see the gray smoke coming out of your mouth. See the expression on your face and any yellowness of your teeth. Feel any harshness in your throat and the way smoking is affecting your body. Ask your lungs if they really want the cigarette and pay particularly close attention to what your lungs are telling you. Chances are the more aware you become of what you are doing, the harder it will be for you to continue.

You can also make smoking more difficult. I have asked clients if they are now only smoking occasionally to smoke only one cigarette from a pack and then give the rest away. Every time they want to smoke, they must go to the store.

Resisting Temptation

The more self-awareness you develop, the more you'll see things worth avoiding which you hadn't before, and things you thought were wrong that aren't. Where our lack of self-understanding and these techniques prove insufficient, this is where our experience comes in. Maybe one day, you'll be really hurt by someone. You'll see that you can never do to someone what has been done to you. You won't have a choice. The effects of your experience will have transformed you. Rather than just following rules or resisting an impulse, you actually change. You see who you are and why you are the way you are. You begin to see the effect your behavior is creating.

This does not take considerable psychological understanding. If you have the intelligence to play cards, follow a movie plot, or become proficient in your native language, your intelligence is sufficient for this endeavor. If you listen to others' conversations, people often pick each others' characters apart with the precision of a brain surgeon. It simply takes a willingness to turn these same powers of perception on ourselves.

We may encounter pain and discomfort sufficient to bring about a change in us. We simply cannot continue in a certain way any longer when the pain has outweighed any incentive to proceed. Often it is fear or denial that restricts us. Once we face these emotions, we see that often the fear was worse than the actuality of what we feared. Through repetition, we *can* reprogram ourselves consciously and subconsciously. Perhaps we develop a new awareness or understanding that allows us to see ourselves differently. Then we can establish a new reaction or relationship with ourselves.

Each one of us is like a puzzle. The mysterious configuration of our life, with its joys, disappointments, dreams, and fears, is the combination that eventually opens the door to our freedom. Everything changes eventually.

If you surrender to God, give up your ego, and stop desiring anything, change will occur in the silence that follows. You will experience true freedom. If you simply do nothing—in the sense that you lie on the sofa all day with all your desires and psychological patterns—change will not happen. But your will, guided by your understanding, can overcome these psychological patterns of the mind. The mind is an instrument of the soul. Like the metaphor of the television we used earlier, a picture appears on the screen. We possess the capacity to change the station. We are the remote controller, the television with all its stations, and the one watching the screen. And just like the television network, it is the programs we choose that are played more often and stay on the air.

Are the meditation exercises we used earlier helpful in developing self-awareness, and inner peace?

Yes. At first, through relaxation you begin to observe your own inner dynamics, to see yourself. This reveals our present nature and character. We must understand ourselves through the mirror of our life and our relationships, and the contents of our own mind through observing and witnessing ourselves. You have to *know* yourself to transcend yourself. How can you be free of something you have become, when you don't know who you are, or how your behavior is affecting you? We are affected unconsciously by impressions from our past, things we are not usually even aware exist within us.

Through deep relaxation, contemplation, and dispassionate observation, you gradually begin to reverse your outward thoughts into an inward awareness of peace, acceptance, and self-understanding.

Church may be helpful. It provides us support, and, it is certainly better to follow rules than to harm someone. However, it is even better to transcend the impulse or need to harm others. If you have not grown beyond real anger and hatred—only suppressed it and pretended not to feel it, and followed the rules of good conduct—you may be someone who is liable to harm someone at the slightest frustration. When we act blindly, unaware of our true motivations, we are a prisoner to our past.

When we become aware of our own thoughts and see ourselves as we are, there is a separation between me and the "me" that is aware of me.

Following a visualization, some people may have the sense they were witnessing something about themselves they are not usually conscious of.

One participant noticed that she felt more observant and relaxed. She described; "It was like I was seeing something true about myself that is probably important. Why am I not usually thinking of this?"

"Why do you think you're not?"

"Well, maybe because if I accept what I saw about myself, I feel like I would have to change. I guess I'm not ready."

"What do you feel would have to happen before you would be ready?"

"I feel I would have to get better grades. Does that sound silly?"

"It doesn't matter what I think. Would you like to use a simple technique to perhaps clarify this question?" "Yes, I would," she responded.

"Okay, if you will, please take a deep breath and hold it for a few seconds. Then exhale slowly through your nose. Focus your attention on an imaginary spot in the center of your forehead, and this time as you exhale say the words "let-go" to yourself. Become aware of your breathing. Now, again, breathe in; hold it, relaxing as you breathe out slowly and "let-go." This time just feel every bit of tension and strain being exhaled out with this next breath. Now, just continue on your own for a few moments. Let your eyes close whenever you choose."

"Very good. Just breathing easily, free from tension, stress, and strain. Feeling comfortable, relaxed and at ease."

"We all have different parts to ourselves. Perhaps a part that likes to be on the go and other times when we just want to relax. There may be times when you think serious, and times when you feel like laughing."

"Now, you have said there is a part of you which is apprehensive about your grades, and feels something else. Is this part willing to communicate with you?" Participant slowly nods her head. "Good, now thank that part for communicating."

"Now, can you increase this signal even more? If you saw a picture in your head, can you make it brighter? If you heard a voice can you make it louder? If you simply had an intuitive feeling, can you increase the intensity of the feeling? You don't need to answer out loud. Gently tap your right index finger once for yes, and twice for no."

She waits a moment, then her finger taps once.

"Very good. Now, ask this part, *what is it trying to do for you? What is it seeking to accomplish?* Now remember, none of our parts mean us any harm, they are each in their own way trying to help us based upon their own experience. Pay exquisite attention to any response; just allow any feelings, words, or pictures to happen. Again, tap your finger when you have seen this." Her finger slowly moves once.

"Now, what do your grades represent? What does it mean to you to get high marks?" Again, she signals with one tap of her finger.

"Now, ask this part, what are two or three things that you can do that will allow this part to feel more comfortable so you can be more relaxed about your grades. Just allow any responses to pop into your head. There are some conditions, however, concerning these suggestions: they must be simple, nothing complicated or confusing. They must be effective, and third, they must be something that you can start right away. Many options may appear at unconscious speeds, so just allow what feels like the three most significant to come to mind. Now, what is the first step that you could take that would make the biggest difference in allowing this part to feel more at ease? Take your time." After a few moments her finger moves very deliberately this time.

"Now, what is the second most important thing that you could do, that would allow this part to feel more comfortable?" Quickly, her finger signals again.

"Now, if there is a third solution, take as much time as you need, what is the next most important step? When you have had enough time, or you have sensed this, just let me know." Her finger signals.

"If this part's previous position was supported by certain concerns, what would it need to feel safe in terms of these changes?" She seems to have a serious look, as her finger signals.

"Do all of your other parts agree with these solutions?" Again, her finger signals once.

"Now, let's move forward in time, through time and space into the future, when in the past you might have been apt to feel a lack of interest in your grades. With these changes in place, are they good enough, do they really work? After a brief pause, her finger signals again.

"Now, is your unconscious mind willing to accept responsibility for generating this new behavior in the appropriate manner, and at the appropriate time?" "Good!"

"See yourself handling this change smoothly and effectively. See your new attitude or course of action, and feel yourself very comfortable and at ease. Notice a look of satisfaction on your face, and your calm confident manner. Listen to the enthusiasm in the voice of others, as they sense these positive feelings in you. Feel a greater sense of confidence and well being, knowing that you have the power to make changes in your life! When you are ready, count from one to five, and open your eyes."

The participant slowly opens her eyes, and has a look as if she was just waking up from a dream; she smiles and says, "That was really neat! I saw that I want to get better grades." Many in the group laugh- as if to say after all that- this was what she had said in the first place.

"Yeah," she continued, "but I saw that before I was letting my parents down by not keeping my grades up. I felt like a failure. Then, when you were asking me questions, I saw that it was ALL my parent's idea! They really wanted me to go to college and major in business. I've been trying to get their approval, and I feel like I'm just going through the motions of college."

"When I really thought about it, I realized that if the choice was totally up to me, I would still go to college, but I wouldn't major in business. One side in me wants to live my own life and make my own decisions. The other side wants to be approved of. But, I know my parents are doing what they think is best for me."

"What did you decide?"

"I saw that I should stay in college, but change my major. My parents might not like it at first, but I think they will go along with it as long as I stay in school and get decent grades."

"When you asked if I needed something to feel safe, I thought of first sitting down with my mom and talking to her, before we talk to my dad."

How Our Past Creates Our Present Problems

When there is an unresolved conflict in our mind, we experience fear, depression, anxiety, anger, and so on. Say, for instance, you have a desire to be loved. As a child, you were constantly reminded of how unlovable you are. This is a conflict. You may seek to be loved, but you may not trust the love you find because you believe you are not deserving of this love. Self-worth is the issue here.

By the same token, if you experienced the trauma of almost drowning as a child, of being submerged under water and not being able to breathe, as an adult you may feel fear every time you're near a body of water. It may not always be practical to stay away from pools, lakes, ponds, and so forth, so here is another conflict.

When there are two emotions or thoughts at odds with each other, one feels anxiety, fear, frustration, and eventually depression. It is this need, however, to integrate our experience that eventually moves us to an awareness of unity.

Through awareness and willingness, we can overcome these conflicts. Some conflicts are just a question of habit, and they are not very deeply rooted. If someone wanted to break a habit of using foul language, for example, he or she would first have to be aware of the behavior. The likely conflict is that the acquired bad language habit is inconsistent with the person's self-image.

More deeply rooted conflicts can be untangled in the same way, in the reverse order as to how the conflict has been created. Whether you are making a conscious effort or not, this process is your life. This is what each of us is learning in our own way, at our own pace. You are doing it now, perhaps. Some people think they are only changing when they are attending a class, reading a book, or consciously making an effort to change. However, every nuance, thought, feeling, dream, idea, hope, pain, experience, is part of your self-actualization. Our journey toward self-understanding is not static, nor does it conform to someone else's formula.

We progress through self-restraint, surrender, and indulgence. At times it is a little more of one or the other. If you are looking for a formula to follow, a set procedure, there are plenty like me who will offer you advice. However, the puzzle that is you has a unique configuration. It takes a special, individualized formula to unlock the door. The key is your life. Do what you feel in your heart is right for you.

Listen to others but learn to listen to your inner voice. Obviously, you are better off avoiding those things that you know are harmful to you or others. That's self-restraint. But don't be against yourself. Work with yourself. Laws are in place if you're unsure. Laws represent the consensus of opinion during a particular time. Manmade laws are not true universally or appropriate for everyone. Our laws today say a person is not eligible to engage in sex until he or she is eighteen years old. Not too long ago, young people were married and started a family by age fifteen or sixteen. In many parts of the world, this is still true today. Surrender yourself to God. Devote your life to the service of the divine. Indulge yourself a little, be kind and appreciate yourself—and don't be too strict.

Freedom and Goals

We all experience a sense of freedom from time to time in our lives, a sense that we are whole, and at peace. We do not need to move a muscle, we are completely content. We are free of any impulse. We can feel a sense of limitlessness, and know everything is fine just the way it is. Achieving this freedom—or at least a greater degree of freedom—you may have to resolve a few issues first.

If your goal is to avoid losing your temper, for example, you might first seek to understand what is at the root of your frustration. Eventually your goal might be to experience a sense of not being the person with the temper, and observing your life as a witness. Then you might find yourself without any goal at all. For example, when doing relaxation techniques, if you are asked to stop thinking, you might think even more in an effort to stop. But if we start by just gradually slowing down our minds, little by little, eventually the mind will quiet. **When is our mind free?**

There is a dimension to everyone's consciousness that has no objectives or needs and is free. This part is always free and does not have to achieve freedom. Another aspect, which possesses the ego, is going through this process to become free and more altruistic. This part is the performer in the play of life. It has assumed a role for the sake of the performance and through its greater consciousness can actually observe itself.

As we experience true freedom, we are drawn to it but limited by our character at the level of our ego. As we strive to be free, our character becomes more altruistic. Even once we dissolve the arbitrary limits of our ego, God may still have a mission for us. Let's say, I wish to simply let go and experience a sense of association with everything, and at the same time, nothing in particular. Don't be surprised if from even this experience, new goals emerge. For example, to help feed the hungry, write a book, community recycling, run for public office, or something. Or you might just sit and watch this fascinating world go around.

Age likely has something to do with one's activity level and turning one's thoughts inward. Some people may lead a very contemplative life even from early childhood. However, often a person only turns to a life of contemplation in their later years after he or she has fulfilled a sense of purpose. Those who grow old without this inner "peace that passes all understanding" may feel very hopeless as their youth and physical energy fades.

Being a Child Again

The scriptures say we should become like a child again. But the point is not to be a child but to become like a child again. The spontaneity and authenticity of children, along with the wisdom of the ages, combine to create marvelous qualities. It doesn't mean to never grow up but to regain certain childlike qualities in the light of our own self-understanding and knowledge.

Children must first learn to see themselves and consider others. Children may be authentic and spontaneous but at an early age they may be self-centered and lack self-perception. A child will grab a toy out of the hands of another child, who will scream and yell while others are trying to talk. Spontaneous as they are, the children may not care much about the experiences of others or the effect their behavior has on others. This must be learned. Some children, unfortunately, pay a very dear price for this education. The child's ego is modified through its interaction. Perhaps, in order to acquire playmates, a child must learn cooperation. It isn't until later, as an adult, we ask the question, "What is beyond the 'me'?"

What happens to our childlike honesty, and authenticity? Have we, in an attempt to negotiate our needs, become cunning, manipulative, clever, and dishonest? This is why it may be necessary for us to become *like* a child again. Even at a very young age, children can learn about themselves. I was with a three-year-old recently, and when I questioned him on the way he was behaving, he got a look on his face like he was caught. He knew—at age three—he was being unreasonable. He smiled and stopped.

It is important to note this education must be done out of kindness. One must be firm but not angry, so as not to crush the child and destroy their ego. To transcend your own ego out of understanding is beautiful. But to be humiliated and abused requires repair. Otherwise, any transcendence will involve a suppression of our wounded ego and lack real joy.

There is a range of stages to this process of self-growth. We each have certain tolerances at different times—it may even vary in the same day. At our lowest level of consciousness, we think and feel mostly in a selfish way. Then at a slightly higher level, we may think occasionally of someone else's feelings. At this lower range, we are prone to greed, prejudice, and envy. If there is inner conflict, we can expect anger, violence, and self-destruction. Most of us feel selfish at least occasionally, and some people act almost exclusively in this range.

Then on our better days, we are friendly, fair, sincere, and kind. We feel in harmony with others and glad to be alive! People who have mastered this level have truly realized how silly greed and anger are. Their whole life then becomes a celebration. They rejoice in existence. Through their unselfishness, the universe smiles on these people. If you act to get attention and give to others for recognition, then your recognition is your happiness. If you give in order to receive, you are bartering with the universe. You truly give when you give without any thought of praise or gain. To give and love, just for the sake of it. "So let each one give as he purposes in his heart, not grudgingly or of necessity; for God loves a cheerful giver." (2 Corinthians 9:7)

Destiny and Freedom

What happens to us after we die? You are you. It's still you at death. You have a consciousness. When you dream, you are experiencing your inner mind. Your consciousness is part and parcel of the collective consciousness. Your consciousness is never unconnected; and your soul is always interconnected. When we die our soul can actually experience another soul, which has passed on. And it can experience a soul that still occupies a body.

Any part of consciousness can be aware of any other part. However, the physical world can only be aware of the physical. For example, your physical eyes can only see something physical. Your consciousness is not limited, however, by the material creation and can have even more vivid and sensual experiences without a body. Imagine that you dream you are in the tropics. You may actually feel the warmth of the sun, smell the ocean breeze, and see the turquoise water—all while you are lying in bed.

You can imagine being many different things, but it is in the physical reality that you become different. Just as in your dreams you may imagine being different, but, it is in your life that changes are made. Until our soul realizes its universal essence and evolves beyond separateness, it comes to earth only due to the nature of its own conception.

I once saw my whole life pass before my eyes, like a movie of highlights. Then it started to fade and amnesia set in. I realized I had taken my own recollection away for the sake of my life. I couldn't live it, nor would I want to live it, if I knew what was always going to happen.

When you experience disturbing dreams, it is because your inner mind is disturbed. If your soul is disturbed, then you must make peace with it. We have all died, just as we have all been born. While in meditation, I have remembered these things.

Hell is terror, fear, our worst despair, grief—the nightmare we wake up from. As we pursue pleasure and happiness, the residue of our experience that is pushed out of our conscious mind and into our unconscious does not disappear. It's like leaving a beautiful affluent part of town and entering the slums. We know it is there, it exists, but we try to ignore it. When we shatter the illusion of our separateness, we see we have created both our pleasure and our pain. Hell, is the result of our unwillingness to accept life unconditionally. If it were not for hell, we would be utterly fooled. Why would we awaken? We would simply live in a romantic illusion of our own imagination, not ever realizing who we really are. Our spirit is the universal consciousness of us all. Within us is the knowledge and understanding of all things. Spiritual awakening is a question of uncovering, or remembering what already lies in our deepest understanding, and what we have fallen asleep to.

Phenomena such as extrasensory perception (ESP), precognition, and out-of-body experiences are studied in parapsychology. These all confirm that the soul or consciousness is not exclusively confined to the body, and the soul is not confined by time. In other words, the soul can exist apart from the body, and the soul is aware of the past, present, and future.

Visions, sightings, and scenes from the future or past are all projections of our own minds. That is not to say they are not accurate, but they are no more important than the observations we make at any given moment. Some people think seeing the future is preferable to seeing the present. If you fail to see the beauty, meaning, and significance in this present moment, then you may think it has to be found in the future, or outside your body.

When a person has a vision, sees the image of a ghost, or knows the future, it can become a preoccupation. If it leads to a holier-than-thou attitude, that person may become derailed from cultivating love and humility and fall into an ego trap.

These experiences may come as a person's awareness develops. However, they may act as an impediment if a person holds them as more significant than genuine kindness, love, friendliness, and compassion shared with others.

Anything that gives us a genuine understanding of ourselves has value. We have all seen the script of our life and have wiped our own recollection away. We know that later, we will not know what's going to happen. Fortune telling reminds me of this example. Have you ever left a coded message for yourself to remind yourself of something? Once I was going to be out of the country for a while. I thought I might not remember my automatic teller bank code number by the time I returned. I didn't want to leave it with my bank card for fear of theft. I made up a code name, "Adam T. Mann," and wrote it on a box, followed by my telephone prefix and my four-digit code. I figured the name would jar my memory and I would realize the significance of the numbers when I saw them again. In the same way, we have designed clues in our life to remind us of certain things. Perhaps, I decided that on a certain day, a certain card, which I will interpret in a certain way, will come up to remind me of something I feel I will need to know.

If on a certain day, someone tells you something important—whether it is a fortune teller or a friend, or your father—it is just that part in the story where you are informing your character by way of another character. Someone else might have a dream or a vision and realize something. Another person is watching the sunset and becomes aware of something important. It is simply a question of whether your preference is for the dramatic, mysterious, or solitary?

Some people say that fortune telling is of the devil. The scriptures tell us that evil is of the devil. Love is of God. Whatever is done in love, including fortune telling, is of God. Ultimately, both love and evil come from God. God created the devil, and the devil could not exist if it were not for God. The devil is just the opposite of the creative force, it's the destructive aspect of God. If you have love, then you must have hate. One has no meaning, without the other. If a story is going to have meaning and be provocative, suspenseful, interesting, adventuresome, you're going to have a varied cast. There are going to be villains, heroes, the weak, the strong, happiness, sadness, and so on.

With prophecy, a tendency can be to think if I can get answers from someone else about what is going on in my life, then why bother trying to understand things for myself? Like all shortcuts, there is a danger here. What if the prophecy for me is biased or a projection of the other person's imagination? For example, let's say a fortune teller tells me I won't be happy for five more years. Will I have the presence of mind to think for myself or will I think blindly in accord with this prediction?

At times a psychic might be helpful if a second opinion is desired to substantiate or clarify one's thoughts. However, beware. In some cases there can be truth mixed in with some fiction. And remember, just because a soul is without a body and speaks through a person, it doesn't mean it is a wise soul.

What about reincarnation? Buddhism teaches that reincarnation does and does not exist. Just as I might think you and I are separate, I might think that my soul will inhabit another body. You and I are really one and the same, ultimately. However, my soul perceives a separation. As long as this separation lasts, my soul can perceive a separate existence and perceive itself as the independent inhabiter of a body. It is, therefore, possible for people to perceive themselves as the inhabiter of many different bodies. The spirit is eternal, unending. Just as it becomes temporarily associated with one body in time, our eternal soul can become infused with another body through another birth. Our soul is ultimately a spirit, without a beginning or end.

It can be born in the world over and over. This sense of separateness can be very persistent. The soul with its subjective conception may survive the body's death and experience itself as various people throughout history.

The soul and the body end in the realm of time. All things end in time, except God and spirit. Beyond time, in timelessness, nothing ends. Timelessness is the nature of spirit. The spirit becomes modified through thought, which is an aspect of time. The soul is a process of thought, however, in essence, is spirit and timeless.

Each of our characters in life usually confines itself to a particular role for the most part, for the sake of the performance. Part of the performance involves people loving each other and experiencing one another as one. This exists for us as a clue to our deeper truth. Through love, we transcend ourselves, our role becomes more altruistic, and we become more loving.

Have you ever read a history book and thought, "What an incredible script?" All the clairvoyance, visions, telepathy, and ESP in the world is worthless if it doesn't increase our capacity to love. It is a part of the play that certain other characters are going to tell each other things about themselves.

Our present conscious awareness began at birth in this life. Our brain cells have recorded data based on stimuli from this life. It is in our inner mind, or unconscious, where past life recollections are discovered. That is what transfers with us from one lifetime to the next. Our soul, with our unconscious mind, is what departs our body at the moment of our death, etched with the impressions left by our character, motives, and intentions. Occasionally, children have past life memories from their unconscious and even act them out in play. At death, our soul disassociates itself from our body, just as we give up our shoes when they are damaged or worn out. Our soul, which is just an aspect of our consciousness, identifies itself with another body at the moment of its birth. This eternal soul does not die with the body. Just as it has become identified with one temporary body, it can, in the same way, identify with another.

If you do not accept rebirth, there can still be a significance for you in these experiences, just as in free association and dream interpretation can also reveal a great deal about the content of a person's unconscious. This knowledge about our unconscious mind can be a very valuable insight for us.

In the Bible there are still some references to rebirth. In the chapter of Matthew, Jesus is said to have gone up on a mountain to pray with Peter, John, and James. The spirits of Moses and Elijah appeared to them. The disciples questioned Jesus, because it was written that Elijah would return to earth during Jesus' time. Jesus replied that Elijah had returned, but people hadn't recognized him. They killed him just as they would one day kill Jesus himself. It says, the men knew Jesus was referring to John the Baptist as the rebirth of Elijah.

Why doesn't Christianity teach that there is reincarnation? It likely did in the past. However, there have been meetings where rulers and bishops have had church records deleted from the Bible that contradict their teachings. Most references to reincarnation were also removed from the Bible, supposedly to give people a greater sense of urgency about their salvation.

The world is like a mirror of all our intentions. When you look at it, you see your own reflection. Your soul is responsible for its future by its own intentions.

God's grace, forgiveness, and mercy can nullify our harmful actions. If you pray to God with a sincere heart and truly feel remorse for the harm you have brought to others, God's mercy can restore our peace. If you show others forgiveness and love, you will receive the same. Likewise, "judge not, so ye be not judged." "Yea shall reap all yea have sown."

During our lives, we usually get quite a lot of feedback from others when we hurt them. Think of someone you know who behaves inappropriately. Has anyone mentioned anything to them? And if so, what was this person's response? Usually, we all have plenty of reminders if we are stepping on someone's toes. But will we listen and change? Often, our life will try to reveal something to us through a plot we happen to be reading in a book or watching in a movie. There may be times when you are listening to someone else discuss their life, and they very accurately describe some element of your own life. We usually receive many clues.

Remember the moral lesson in the Christmas story, *A Christmas Carol?* Didn't people try to tell Scrooge he was a grump? In the beginning, did he care? The key for Scrooge lies first in an awareness of himself, then in a willingness to change.

Ultimately, we do have free will. Relatively speaking, we don't. We are characters in God's script. God is free and not bound by its own creation. Through God giving each of us life, we each have a relationship with God. Through God's grace and mercy, all things are possible.

Many writers have said their own characters have come to life for them, as if they have personalities of their own. They even come to love and care for each of the characters they have created.

Imagine you are a cartoonist and your comic strip appears daily in the newspaper. You are the creator of the cartoon, and illustrate and narrate all the events. Are your characters themselves free? What will of their own do they actually have? Can a character chose to do what it wants, independent of you, the cartoonist? No. The character relies on the script that you write. Each character appears to have a personality of its own. We come to know the character and even anticipate what might happen in the following day's cartoon. Is the cartoonist obligated to write the cartoon in a certain way? No. The creator of the script can write the cartoon as he or she wishes. The cartoonist may have an idea of how the plot will unfold for some time to come or even have the whole series thought out ahead.

For example, perhaps, the cartoonist can see in his or her mind the events each character will be involved in the following week. Let's say one of the characters will fly a kite in a thunderstorm. But if the cartoonist decides to change this prior to publication, it can be done. Chances are, however, what the cartoonist writes will be consistent with the evolution of that character and make sense in light of all that has transpired previously.

God is the master cartoonist and has written the whole series. God is aware of the script for our lives and knows what will happen to us. However, God can change the script at any moment, on a whim, and still he knows what is going to happen.

It is as though you can write many different endings for a particular story, and perhaps, you have one particular ending in mind. If you change your mind, you still know how it will end at the moment you decide. That is why, even if someone is a great psychic, he or she cannot tell you with absolute certainty what is going to happen. Any fate, no matter how probable, can be transcended through God's grace.

Here is the secret: The character is ultimately free. Because who is the character? The character and the cartoonist are none other than the same. How can you separate the two? If I draw a cartoon, don't you acknowledge the cartoon as mine? When you meet me, don't you think of me and my cartoon character as one and the same? You think of my characters as free, because you know I can draw them doing anything I want. Once a character realizes its identity, as an actual manifestation of a free Supreme Being, what can then bind them? When we pray, we are communicating with what is divine within us. Therein lies an infinite number of story lines and endings. Through this recognition we are free!

So do we have any real life of our own? Yes we do, in the same way any character has life. Everyone who reads the cartoon feels something for each character. The character takes on a life of its own. Even the cartoonist feels the characters have a life of their own. The creator is amused and delighted and feels a great deal for each of its created beings. What is the character's real identity in relationship to all the other players? No one has supremacy over anyone else. Can you imagine one cartoon character saying to another, "I am superior to you"? How silly. We are all created equal in God's eyes.

What About Science and Religion?

Science tells us our first living systems formed from a cloud of dust, swirling in God's gravitational whirlpool. From this has evolved all the variety that we see in our universe today.

It's an old question: Which came first, the chicken or the egg?

She was a cold-blooded reptile with scales, who laid this egg, that grew into a creature with feathers. After many, many generations, this animal became known as a chicken.

The changes in life are inevitable, but there is a chemistry to the inherent nature of things. Spirit is the presence of the unlimited God in each of us. Spirit is the potential form of the individual soul. In the individual soul, there is manifested on the physical dimension an energy that supplies the mental and emotional aspects of one's life. This represents the potential of the body's energy, which supplies the body's activity. In this relationship between the mental and physical, you can use one to affect the other. Have you noticed, when you are enthusiastic, how much more you get done? Or have you ever experienced a runner's high that affects your mental status?

Our nervous system is the body's information-gathering, storage, and control system. The central processing unit is the central nervous system, which comprises the brain and spinal cord, consisting of billions of interconnecting nerve cells. Energy passes through the central nerve, connecting the base of the spine with the brain at the top of the head. In Eastern religion they teach there are seven major centers along this path and as this energy rises you can experience an expansion and elevation of your awareness. When we are aware of our energy, especially in certain areas of our body, we can experience a release from our more subjective thoughts. As a concentration of this energy rises up from the base of the spine, it intensifies our experiences at certain points along the way. For example, when we say we have a "gut feeling" about something, this corresponds to a primary energy center that is located in the area of our solar plexus. When we say we feel our "heart melting," this relates to the area that corresponds to our heart.

Love for God, devotion, prayer, faith, truth, and kindness act as the most powerful means to raise up one's consciousness. Songs, joy, singing, and sounds are very influential. Both sound and light are expressions of consciousness and automatically less dense than the physical body. Sound vibration and awareness are very close in a sense. Certain sound frequencies correspond to the awareness of unity and freedom, which can escape the understanding of even the most intelligent. When an intense realization occurs, the mind is released from its separateness and experiences the universal spirit as the essence of everything.

Is our perception of diversity, then, just a question of our senses? Physically, yes. But consciousness is also polarized for us, most of the time. Our universe exists for us, polarized, between hot and cold, solid and gas, positive and negative particles, and so on. Through opposites, the infinite takes form. However, synchronization exists between all separate things: a universal, multilevel, systematic interrelationship. This is the hidden significance behind such things as astrology and numerology. Systems form as subsystems of other systems. Each particular atom, molecule, organism, star, integer, and so on behaves in a certain way, relative to its system's relationship to each other system. There is a direct correlation between one system and another.

For example, grunion fish spawn on the beach in the spring when the full moon coincides with the highest tide of the month. The fish don't know intellectually when this is. They are responding to an interrelated cycle, inherent in themselves and in the ecological and astronomical systems of the universe—in this case, the moon's relationship to the earth and the time of year. We observe an apparent characteristic as being separate. But when viewed in a more expansive way, its characteristics cannot be considered independent from all other surrounding influences.

On a conscious level, this polarity creates for us what we prefer and what we avoid. By our individual nature, our destiny is created.

The Bible, of course, doesn't mention evolution. Nor does it discuss the shape of the earth, its orbit around the sun, chromosomes, mitosis, the nature of atomic particles, continental drift, electricity, X-rays, and so on. The Bible is an incomplete account of science as we know it today. After all, two thousand years of research has been conducted. As far as love and God go, nothing has changed.

A knowledge of archaeology and biology was not a prime concern in biblical times. The concept of a billion years—or a billion anything—was probably inconceivable. As the cosmos formed, God ultimately remained undifferentiated, while also sending an infinitesimal part of its infinite self into space. Science tells us that lightning energy electrified an eddy that eventually became our earth. Hydrogen and helium formed as it cooled and passed through various stages. All this was orchestrated by God.

There are many references to the stars in the Bible. In Psalms 19:1 it says, "The heavens declare God's glory, and reveal the work of his hands." Jesus' birth was located by the wise men from the East, who followed a star. We are told that certain events will occur when we see certain signs in the heavens.

Drug Use and Spirituality

Drugs vary greatly in their effects, as well as the reasons people have for using them. Many kids turn to drugs because they are looking for something that is missing from their lives, and they don't know how to find it. The opiates, or narcotic drugs, are generally for escaping difficulties.

The psychoactive, or psychedelic drugs, have been used for their consciousness-altering effects. Many cultures throughout the ages have used certain plants with mind-altering properties in their religious rites and to communicate with the spiritual realms. In most nonindustrial societies the hallucinogenic plants have been considered sacred and have been used in many religious ceremonies. Native Americans in several regions of the United States took the peyote cactus. Various plants have long been recognized—before LSD—for heightening awareness and revealing the inner compartments of one's mind.

Today as well as in the past, these drugs present a very real hazard when used by unsuspecting people who are troubled or emotionally and psychologically distraught, and not for the purpose of serious spiritual inquiry. Drug use has provided a means of escape from fear and despair for many, although much less so from the hallucinogens. And certainly, there are those who have had fierce and negative emotions released from their unconscious minds, which brought harm and injury to themselves and others. These powerful psychological affects are not for the weak-willed, feeble, or confused who lack spiritual conviction—or those harboring suppressed fears and resentments, unless they are prepared to face them.

For some, this escape has led straight into a living nightmare. Others have found a world where visions were shaped by their inner minds and brought to life in a way that would mystify even the experts in motion picture special effects. Some see themselves and their character and nature reflected on the mirror of their inner awareness. What wonderful or gruesome images lie in wait for the unsuspecting. Those who have had courage enough to take a glimpse may be unprepared for these images within themselves, while some are delightfully rewarded with the vision of true freedom—a transcendence beyond their ego and phenomenal life, to realms scarcely imagined. Others, who fear what might lie hidden inside themselves, do so with good reason.

Imagine the surprise of an early man who ate a plant or some fungi, then saw a ghost or a departed relative? Stranger still, must have been the occurrence of seeing the future, being able to read someone else's mind, or experiencing the vivid impressions of their own subconscious. Is it any wonder that many cultures hailed these substances as divine?

Don't you think all drugs are just an escape? In a sense, yes. But for some people this is not a bad thing, when it is their prejudices, bias, or misconceptions they are escaping from. There you go, mixing up the truth again. Whose truth?

Aren't these all just hallucinations? No.

When I was quite young, I started seeing ghosts and had several out-of-body experiences that were completely non-drug related. When I was about nine years old, my deceased grandfather appeared to me, and I actually heard him speak. I reluctantly mentioned this to my father and he told me I had quite an active imagination. I knew what I had seen was as real as anything else, and later I spent many years searching to discover explanations for what I had experienced. Since then, I have met many people who have had similar experiences.

UFOs, ESP, and Voodoo?

What we imagine is what exists for us, isn't it? Imagination does not simply refer to only dreams but, to some extent, to all the thoughts you have as a result of your consciousness. Because what we imagine to exist is almost entirely a result of our own personal interpretations of our world, and this isn't existence itself. We may experience our consciousness as a thought, feeling, dream, physical event, vision, and so on. This is only our own subjective interpretation of existence. And at our most spiritual level of consciousness, this includes even imagining we have a body and a separate life in the first place. Everything we subjectively conceive of is represented in whatever form or frequency it corresponds to in our physical, mental, and spiritual worlds. For example, a radio wave cannot be seen by your eyes but that doesn't mean it doesn't exist. Someone had to first even imagine the possibility of a radio before we had one. Until then, many would have said that a box you can hear invisible people and songs from is simply a fantasy.

Our consciousness includes that which we call physical and nonphysical—and everything in between. Some things are subtle, such as air or gas. Other things are dense, such as iron or lead. Think of the difference between one square foot of air verses one square foot of iron. Then, there are many degrees of existence even more subtle than gas or air. Take a ghost, for example.

It exists but not in the same density as your body, or even a cloud.

Unidentified flying objects (UFOs) are being talked about more and more often. Centuries ago, few people probably thought very much about them. There were rarely recorded sightings in those days. As our thoughts about them have increased, we are actually drawing them out and into our consciousness.

Wouldn't it be exciting if there were a space alien here, in our midst? I'm sure it would take us all by surprise, regardless of how often we have thought about them. It would be exhilarating, like seeing a fascinating sight. Think of how this experience might cause us to look at ourselves and our universe differently. Unfortunately, all too often, the things we find fascinating at first soon become commonplace. Eventually, we stop really looking or seeing any longer. Think about how we treat most other species. Fortunately, there is a growing awareness today of the necessity to treat all creatures kindly, especially those that are endangered.

There are those who may have had an experience they can't explain without learning more about UFOs. When something we experience doesn't fit into our understanding of our world, it often creates the necessity for us to explore the experience further, to bridge the gap.

Some people who have not experienced UFO's are also very fascinated by them and spend a lot of time talking about them. In general, if a person does not really feel involved with the people and everyday aspects of their lives, they often look for things to distract themselves. The "why" we are interested in something is the real question. What we call the "supernatural" is our clue that there is more to this existence than meets our present awareness. Unexplained phenomena in our lives often point the way toward further investigation.

Sometimes these subjects may become an escape for someone. If it provides us with an excuse to ignore the current issues of our life, then we know we may be using it to avoid something we don't want to face. It is easy to declare oneself an "authority" on UFOs. Who's going to say who's accurate when it comes to understanding aliens? Often when we are bored with our life, it is because we have developed a sense of isolation and may have pushed others away. Usually, we isolate ourselves out of fear or resentment. When people feel alone, they often begin to think almost all the time about themselves and their own problems. Before long, others begin to lose interest in them because they may feel this person has become too self-absorbed. It is then this person is apt to become preoccupied with some extraneous event or interest to add significance to their life, perhaps to distract themselves from their loneliness.

Although some may question the right- or wrongness of delving into the supernatural, it all depends on why you are interested. I recently spoke with a woman who had a strong desire to talk with her deceased mother. She held seances, hired psychics, and spent a great deal of energy and money trying to communicate with her. She asked me if I thought it was wrong. Out of curiosity, I asked her if she and her mother had been very close. She said, "No, not really. We had a falling-out, and we didn't speak to each other very much toward the end of my mother's life." Why is it we don't take the chance to communicate more often with others while we are focused in the same dimension they are? And why do some people place a greater significance on speaking to an alien or a ghost, than to their own friends and neighbors?

In the matter of black magic, voodoo, and people who cast spells, the Eastern scriptures say, if we believe ourselves to be vulnerable or deserving of punishment, there are those who will gladly punish us. An attack is an assault, whether it is from someone you meet face to face or someone's voodoo, spell, or whatever else. A spell can't be cast on someone unless they are susceptible to it, because of their own fate.

Either way, the one who even trys to cast an evil spell is going to bring harm to themselves.

Sometimes trouble comes to us to teach us something, like compassion or trust. Other times we may have brought consequences upon ourselves because of our own actions. Sometimes guilt brings someone into our life who is more than willing to punish us. There are many people who are willing to hurt you, if you think you deserve it.

Have you ever been in an unsafe place? Doesn't it cause you to suspect that it is best to avoid the wrong people whenever possible? I wouldn't worry about evil spirits, whether they presently have a body or not. I would avoid them though. There are great evils in the spirit world, just like in our physical world.

If you direct your thoughts toward God and goodness, it is like exposing mold to sunlight. Evil cannot exist in the light of love and God. Imagine ignorance and evil are like a dark cave. No matter how many centuries the cave has been dark, once you enter with a lantern the darkness is instantly dispelled. The light doesn't have to struggle or try to force the darkness out. Darkness is the absence of light. Remember this whenever you encounter evil. Your light, or devotion, is your protection. Always direct your thoughts toward God and love.

REFERENCES

[1] The Beatles, *White Album*. EMI Records Ltd., 1968

[2] M. K. Krishnan, *Gandhi Speaks: Selections from his writings*. Navajivan Press

[3] Brian L. Weiss, M.D. *Many Lives Many Masters*. New York: Simon & Schuster, 1988

[4] Kahlil Gibran, *The Prophet*. New York: Alfred A. Knopf, 1927

[5] Misty Flatt, *Religion*. Dana Point: The Chela Journal, April 1997, pp 3

[6] Neil A. Campbell, Ph.D, *Biology*. The Benjamin/Cummings Publishing Company, 1993

[7] Rabbi Joshua Liebman, *Peace of Mind*. Oxford, 1945

[8] Norman Vincent Peale, *Power of Positive Thinking*. Prentice Hall, 1954

[9] Napoleon Hill, *Think and Grow Rich*. New York: Ballantine Books, 1960

[10] Yogi Bhajan, *Physical Wisdom*. Los Angeles: Kundalini Research Institute, 1994

[11] Satguru Sivaya Subramuniyaswami, *Dancing With Siva*. Kapaa, Hawaii: Himalayan Academy, 1993

[12] *The Holy Bible*, New York: International Bible Society, 1978

[13] Nikhilananda, Swami, *The Gospel of Sri Ramakrishna*. New York: Ramakrishna-Vivekananda Center, 1958

[14] Yogi Ramacharaka, *The Spirit of the Upanishads*. Chicago: The Yogi Publication Society, 1907

[15] Eknath Easwaran, *The Bhagavad Gita*. Petaluma, CA: Nilgiri Press, 1985

[16] Raymond Moody, M.D., *Life After Life*. New York: Mockingbird Books, 1975

[17] Deepak Chopra, M.D., *Quantum Healing*. New York: Bantam Books, 1989

[18] Eknath Easwaran, *The Bhagavad Gita*. Petaluma, CA: Nilgiri Press, 1985

[19] *The Holy Bible*, New York: International Bible Society, 1978

INDEX

A

Abortion, 89-90
Absolute, 27, 65
Actualization, 80
Age, 109
  of Pisces, 14
Aliens, 16, 126-127
All unique, 73
Animals, 90-91
Aquarius, 14-16
Astrology, 14-16, 19, 120, 121
Atoms, 27, 84
Aura, 64
Awareness, 101, 107
  Self, 69, 102
  Spontaneous, 71
  Subjective, 70

B

Bad habits, 100
Being a child again, 109-110
Being and nonbeing, 79
Beliefs, 82
Bhagavad Gita, 54, 61-62
Bhakti, 37-38
Bible, 88, 92, 121
Black holes, 80-81

Bodhidharma, 26-27
Body, 120
  and brain, 25, 62
  as frequency, 59-60
Brain, 40-41
Brain frequency, 69
Brain waves, 72-73
Breath counting, 38
Bully on the block, 87

C

Cartoonist, 117-118
Chakras, 54
Change, 99, 101-102
Children, 109-110
Chopra, Dr. Deepak, 59
Christianity, 116
Church, 102
Condemning, 53
Conflict, 106, 107
Consciousness, 65, 70, 79, 111, 125
  collective, 70, 71, 111
  expansive, 70
  frequency, 69
  impartial, 71
  internal, 71

states of, 72
universal, 70
Creation, physical, 111
laws of, 75

D

Darkness, 128
Death, 111
Death penalty, 87
Destiny, 22, 111-112
Devil, 114
Devotion, 120
Devotional energy, 48
Diversity, 78, 120
DNA, 77
Dollar bill, 11
Dreams, 69, 111-112
Drugs, 122-123
    LSD, 122
    Spirituality, 122

E

Eastern religion, 9
Eating animals, 90-91
    Bible, 92
    Native Americans, 91
Ego, 7, 80, 83, 86, 79, 108
    child's, 101, 109, 110
Egoless, 80
Electroencephalograph, 73 (EEG).
Elijah, 116
Emotions, 107
End of the world, 12-14
Energy, 80, 120
    and Spirit, 65
    field of, 79
    unity of, 72
Energy frequency, 111
Enlightenment, 33
Enter the kingdom, 82
ESP, 112, 115

Essence is the same, 74, 86
Everything, 79
    one, 18
Evolution, 117-118, 121
    Stellar, 71
Existence, 26, 78-80, 125-126
    becomes conscious, 80
    experience the infinite, 80

F

Faith, 120
Fana, 43
Flesh and bones, 65
Fortune telling, 113-115
Freedom, 17, 78, 108-109
Freemasons, 10-11
Freewill, 117-118
Fulfillment, 78

G

Galaxies, 84
Getting lost, 77
Ghosts, 58-60, 123, 125, 127
Gibran, Kahlil, 6-7
Goals, 108
God, 26, 49, 61, 75-83, 99, 101, 128
    and nonexistent, 79
    beyond the existent, 79
    communicate with, 76
    consciousness, 65
    created all things, 78
    creation itself, 79
    experiences itself, 80
    formless, 65
    is the rock, 78
    love, 46
    lover of, 31
    presence, 22
    realized person, 30
    script, 117
    service to, 23

Index

Great Spirit, 43

H

Hallucinations, 123
Hell, 112
Hierarchy of needs, 20
Holy Spirit, 23, 76, 89
Homosexuality, 95
Human brain, 40
Hypnosis, 5, 115
  past life, 62

I

Imagination, 125
Indulgence, 108
Inner nature, 77
Inner space, 84
Inner voice, 107
Insecurity, 78
Integrate, 41
Intention, 89
Interpretations, 125

J

Jesus, 19, 82-83, 89, 116, 121
John the Baptist, 83, 116

K

Kali Yuga, 12-14
Karma Yoga, 17-18
Killing, 47, 88
Kirlian camera, 64
Koan, 30
Krishna, 54, 61-62
Krishnamurti, 3, 26
Kundalini, 4, 52
  Yoga, 4

L

Laws, 107
Liberation, 18

Life, 119
  after death, 57
  laws, 70
  like a puzzle, 101
  meaning of, 71-72
  on earth, 119
  on other planets, 63
Light, 120, 128
Love, 93
  falling in, 96-97
  making, 49-51
  yourself, 77

M

Maasauu, 43
Maheshh, Maharishi, 3
Male and female, 49
Mantra, 37
Marriage, 93-94, 95, 96
Maslow, Dr. Abraham, 20-21
Mass destruction, 10
Material success, 21
Mayans, 13
Meaning of life, 71-72
Meditation, 5, 29-31, 33-44
  breath counting, 38-39
  concentrating, 37-38
  eyes open, 38
  gradually increase, 44
  helpful hints, 36-37
  naturally occurring, 39
  once ready, 35
  position, 34
  religion, 41
  restlessness, 39
  therapy as, 40
  time table, 44
  Zen, 39
Mercy, 116
Millennium, 9, 25
Mind, 69
  like a lake, 34

like a snowball, 70
makes a decision, 70
mindfulness, 36
Moody, Dr. Raymond, 57-58
Morality, 85-91
    changing, 87
    necessity, 85
Music, 120

N

Namaste, 8
Near death experience (NDE), 57-58
Needs, 21
Nervous system, 53
Neuro-linguistic Programming (NLP), 25-26, 29
New Age, 3, 5, 10-11, 21, 45
Nothingness, 80-81
Nuclear bomb, 10
Numerology, 120

O

Observing, 102
    dispassionate, 71, 102
Omnipotent, 75
Omnipresent, 75, 78, 80
Oneness, 43
Other planets, 63
Other space, 84
Our past, 106
Outlook, 69
Out of body, 112, 123

P

Parts, spiritual, 76
Past lives, 5, 60-63
    investigation into, 62
Perspective, 72
Piscean Age, 19
Pisces, 14

Play that part, 76
Positive and negative, 79
Prana, 48
Prayer, 76-77, 81
Precognition, 112
Present problems, 106
Previous lives, 6, 115
Prophesies, 14
    different aspects, 82
    like scuba diving, 82
Prophet, 42
    different beliefs, 82
    not a, 42
    thought to be crazy, 42
Psychic, 70, 114, 118
Punishment, 127-128

Q

Question everything, 83-84
Quieting the mind, 33

R

Ramakrishna, 30-31
Reality, 27-28, 79-80
    infinite number of, 27
Real you, 60
Red giants, 71
Reflection, 71
Reincarnation, 114-115
Relaxation, 102, 108
Religion, 116
    goal of, 81
    why, 81
    variations in, 81-82
    repetition, 101
Right or "good," 7, 102
Rosicrucians, 49

S

Sacrifice, 83
Samadhi, 41-43

Index

Satisfaction, 78
Satorti, 43
Satya Yuga, 12
Savikalpa, 41
Science and religion, 119-122
Scrooge, 117
Seances, 127
See, 71
Self-actualization, 21
Self-control, 47-48
Self-growth, 99
   stages, 110
Self-realization, 18, 21
Self-restraint, 107
Self-surrender, 19, 101
Self-understanding, 77, 102-103, 106
Sensory pleasure, 78
   me, 86
Separateness, 86, 114
Sex, 45, 94-96
   before marriage, 94-95
   breathing, 50
   drive, 48
   growth, 95
   integration, 51
   stages, 110
   premarital, 93
   negativity, 96
   spiritualized, 45
   tantric, 49-50
Sexes, 49-50
Significance, 83
Slavery, 86
Smoking, 100
Somewhere, 71
Soul, 60, 76, 78, 111, 114
Sound, 120
Space,
   inner, 84
   outer, 84
Spells, 127

Spirit, 7, 17, 78-79, 114, 119
Spiritual existence, 17
Spiritual laws, 116
Spontaneous awareness, 71
Srimad Bhagavatam, 63
Stars, 80
Star Trek, 26
Stellar evolution, 71
Subconscious mind, 69
Subjective
   experience, 71
   outlook, 70
Supernatural, 126-127
Supreme intelligence, 75
Surrender, 83, 108
Synchronization, 120

T

Tantra Yoga, 45-55
Tantric philosophy, 53-55
Tao, 52
Teachers, 71
Telepathy, 115
Temptation, 101
Thoughts stop, 70
Time, 79-81
Timelessness, 81
Transcend ourselves, 22, 85-86, 109
Transmutation, 46, 51
Trouble, 128
Truth, 65

U

UFO, 126-127
Unconscious, 65, 79
Understanding, 101
Unified whole, 19
Universal, 120
   consciousness, 70
Universe, 84

Unselfishness, 110
Upadesaahasri, 43
Upanishads, 21-22, 43

V

Vasanas, 29
Vegetarianism, 90-91
Visions, 112
Visualization, 105
    Guided, 103-105
Voo doo, 127-128

W

Wealth, 21
White dwarfs, 71
Why are we born, 111

Witnessing, 72, 103
    within us, 70
World
    end of the, 12-14
    periods, 11
    problems, 89

Y

Yin and Yang, 53
Yoga, 47
Yugas, 11
Yukteswarji, Swami Sri, 16

Z

Zen, 25-30, 39

Give the Gift of
ZERO POINT
Moments Beyond Conscious Thought
to Your Friends and Colleagues

CHECK YOUR LEADING BOOKSTORE OR ORDER HERE

www.new-age.org

❑ **YES**, I want _____ copies of ***Zero Point: Moments Beyond Conscious Thought*** $12.95 each, plus $3 shipping per book (California residents please add $1.00 sales tax per book). Canadian orders must be accompanied by a postal money order in U.S. funds. Allow 15 days for delivery.

❑ **YES**, I am interested in having the author, or one of your other gifted presenters, give a seminar to my company, association, school or organization. Please send information.

My check or money order for $ _____ is enclosed.
Please charge my: ❑ Visa   ❑ MasterCard

Name _____

Address _____

City/State/Zip _____

Phone _____

Card # _____

Exp. Date _____ Signature _____

Please make your check payable and return to:
Innersights
P.O. Box 3625
Dana Point, CA 92629

Call your credit card order to: 800-983-4445